# A BRIEF HISTORY OF WALT DISNEY

Dreams, Animation, and Innovation: Crafting the Magic of Disney and Shaping Entertainment History

## SCOTT MATTHEWS

# Contents

*"Get a good idea, and stay with it. Dog it, and work at it until it's done, and done right."*

*- Walt Disney*

# Introduction

Walt Disney stands as one of the most iconic and influential figures in the history of entertainment, a visionary who transformed the world with his imagination and innovation. His journey from modest beginnings to creating a global empire is a testament to his relentless determination, creativity, and entrepreneurial spirit. *A Brief History of Walt Disney* chronicles the extraordinary life of Walt Disney, tracing his path from a small house on Tripp Avenue to becoming a beloved household name and the architect of a cultural legacy that continues to enchant generations.

Disney's story is rooted in his early experiences within a diverse family background. The fourth son of Elias Disney, an Irish-Canadian, and Flora Call Disney, an American of German and English descent, Walt grew up in a household that valued hard work, perseverance, and creativity. These principles, imparted by his stern yet industrious father and his nurturing, supportive mother, shaped Walt's character and fueled his artistic aspirations.

From a young age, Disney displayed a remarkable talent for drawing and storytelling. His passion for art blossomed on his family's farm in Marceline, Missouri, where he sketched farm animals and created his first rudimentary animations. The bond with his brother Roy and his partnership with fellow artist Ub Iwerks were instrumental in his early ventures, leading to the creation of beloved characters and setting the stage for his future successes.

Walt Disney's career was marked by both triumphs and trials. The loss of his creation: Oswald the Lucky Rabbit to Charles Mintz was a significant setback that tested his resolve but also spurred him to create Mickey Mouse. Mickey's debut in *Steamboat Willie*, the first synchronized sound cartoon, revolutionized animation and established Disney as a pioneering force in the industry. This period of innovation was characterized by Disney's ability to merge technical advancements with compelling storytelling, captivating audiences worldwide.

Disney's relentless pursuit of excellence led to the creation of Disneyland in 1955, a groundbreaking theme park that became a magical haven for families. His visionary contributions to the 1964 New York World's Fair, including the enduring "It's a Small World" attraction, showcased his commitment to creating immersive experiences that blended entertainment with educational value.

This book delves into the life of Walt Disney, exploring the milestones, innovations, and personal moments that defined his journey. It offers a comprehensive look at the man behind the magic, whose imagination and creativity have left an indelible mark on the world. Through his story, we gain insight into the mind of a true visionary whose contributions to entertainment continue to inspire and captivate audiences around the globe.

# The Early Years: The Beginnings of a Dreamer

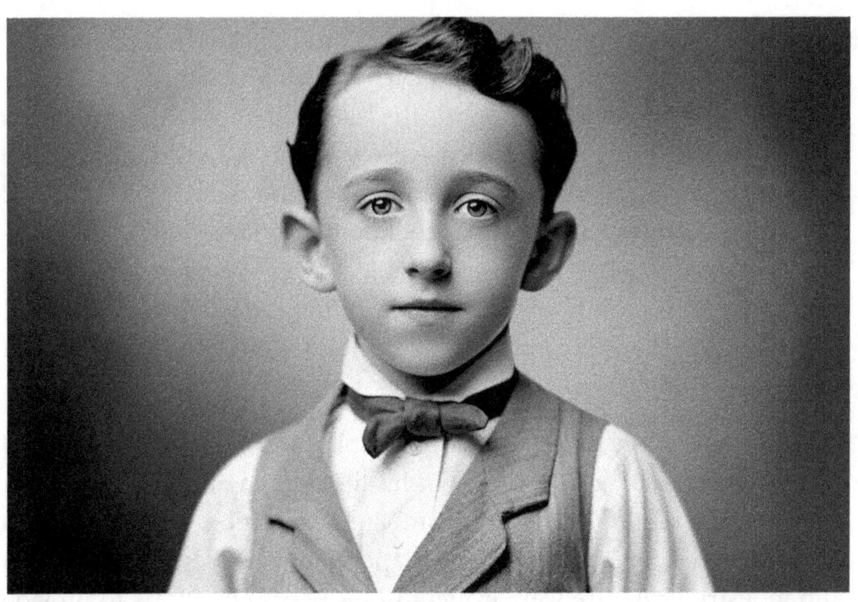

Walt Disney, the creative genius behind one of the most influential entertainment empires in history, was born on December 5, 1901, at 1249 Tripp Avenue, in Chicago's Hermosa neighborhood. This modest beginning was the start of a journey that would see Walt transform the world of entertainment and become a beloved household name. His lineage traced back to Jean Christophe D'Isigny, who accompanied William the Conqueror in 1066. The family name, originally D'Isigny, was anglicized to Disney. Though the Disneys were conquerors in England, they later became simple farmers in Ireland. In 1834, a branch of the Disney family emigrated to America. Walt's father, Elias Disney, was a carpenter working on a church project for Pastor Walter Parr, who inspired Elias to name his son Walter Elias Disney.

Walt was the fourth son of Elias Disney, an Irish-Canadian who had emigrated from Canada, and Flora Call Disney, an American of German and English descent. Their marriage was a union of diverse cultural backgrounds that would play a part in shaping the values and perspectives of their children.

The Disney family included Walt's older brothers Herbert, Raymond, and Roy, each of whom had their own roles within the family dynamic. Herbert and Raymond, the eldest, took on responsibilities early, often helping their father with various tasks to support the family. Roy, closer in age to Walt, would become not just a sibling but a lifelong business partner and confidant. In December 1903, the family was completed with the birth of Walt's younger sister, Ruth. The close-knit nature of the Disney family, despite the financial struggles they faced, provided a strong foundation of love and support.

Elias Disney was a man of stern principles and a strong work ethic. He held a series of jobs throughout his life, ranging from construction work at the 1893 World's Columbian Exposition in Chicago to farming and later running a newspaper route. Elias's determination and industrious nature were evident in his persistent efforts to provide for his family, no matter the adversity they faced. This relentless drive for self-improvement and financial stability left a lasting impression on young Walt, teaching him the value of hard work and perseverance.

Flora Call Disney, on the other hand, balanced Elias's stern demeanor with her nurturing and supportive approach. She was a homemaker who ensured that her children received a well-rounded upbringing, filled with love and encouragement. Flora's gentle influence helped in cultivating Walt's imaginative mind and creative talents from an early age. She recognized and fostered his artistic inclinations, encouraging him to pursue his interests even when times were tough. Her role in the family was crucial, providing a sense of stability and warmth that would be a source of comfort for Walt throughout his life.

The Disney household, though modest, was rich in moral values and a strong sense of community. Family gatherings, storytelling sessions, and shared responsibilities were the norm. These early experiences in a supportive and industrious household imbued Walt with a sense of duty, creativity, and an appreciation for the simple joys of life.

In addition to the influence of his immediate family, the neighborhood of Hermosa itself played a significant role in shaping Walt's early years. It was a vibrant community where children could explore, play, and dream. The close-knit nature of the neighborhood allowed for a sense of belonging and security for the children. The Disney family's modest house on Tripp Avenue was often filled with the sounds of Elias working on one project or another, while Flora tended to the household chores with care and precision.

In 1903, the Disney family left Chicago due to dissatisfaction with city life and Elias Disney's gambling debts. They moved to Marceline, Missouri, where Elias worked on his brother Robert's apple farm. By 1906, Elias had saved enough to buy forty acres (1,742,400 square feet or 161,874 square meters) and started his own apple farm, with help from his sons. In 1909, Raymond and Herbert left, leaving more work for Roy and Walt. Elias became stricter, causing Walt to rely more on his mother Flora for comfort and inspiration.

Marceline would become a significant place for Walt, as it was here that he first developed a passion for drawing. One of the pivotal moments in Walt's early artistic development occurred when he was about nine years old. A retired neighborhood doctor, Dr. Sherwood, recognized Walt's budding talent and, impressed by the young boy's enthusiasm and skill, commissioned him to draw his horse, Rupert. For Walt, this was more than just a drawing assignment; it was a validation of his talent and a significant boost to his confidence. The joy and satisfaction he derived from this task ignited a deep, lifelong love for art and drawing. Walt later mentioned this event in an interview as, "I was going to draw a picture of Rupert for him and he was going to give me a nickel. He got Rupert out and being a stallion was very restless."

Walt's passion for drawing soon became an integral part of his daily life. He would spend countless hours practicing his craft, often sitting under a tree or by the barn, with a sketchpad in hand. His subjects ranged from farm animals and local characters to imaginary scenes and fantastical creatures, all brought to life by his vivid imagination and keen observational skills.

To further hone his abilities, Walt began copying the cartoons from the front page of the *Appeal to Reason* newspaper, a socialist publication that

his father subscribed to. The cartoons, often satirical and politically charged, were created by notable cartoonists like Ryan Walker. These illustrations provided Walt with valuable lessons in caricature, expression, and storytelling through images. He meticulously studied each drawing, learning how to convey complex emotions and narratives with simple yet effective lines.

His mother, Flora, and his older brother, Roy, were particularly supportive, often admiring his drawings and encouraging him to keep at it. This familial support was vital, as it reinforced the value of his artistic endeavors and motivated him to continue improving his skills.

The natural surroundings of Marceline also fueled Walt's creativity. The rolling hills, lush fields, and vibrant wildlife provided a picturesque backdrop for his drawings. Walt would often venture out with his sketchbook, capturing the essence of the rural environment in his art. The tranquility and beauty of Marceline's landscapes fostered a deep appreciation for nature, which would later be reflected in many of his animated works, where lush, detailed settings became a hallmark of Disney films.

Living near the Atchison, Topeka, and Santa Fe Railway line, Walt became fascinated with trains, a theme that would later be visible in his creative works. The rhythmic chugging and the whistle of the trains sparked his imagination, embedding a sense of adventure and movement in his psyche. This early enchantment with locomotives can be seen in various aspects of his later creations, most notably the Disneyland Railroad.

In late 1909, Walt and his sister Ruth started their formal education at the Park School in Marceline. The Disney family were active members of their local Congregational church, where Walt's sense of community and moral values were nurtured. These formative experiences in a close-knit, rural setting contributed to the themes of community and family that would later be evident in his work.

After contracting pneumonia, Elias sold the farm in 1909 and moved the family to Kansas City to manage a large newspaper delivery route, anticipating better financial returns in the bustling newspaper industry. Here Walt started attending Benton Grammar School, where he met Walter Pfeiffer, a fellow student whose family introduced Walt to the world of vaudeville* and motion pictures. Walt spent more time at the Pfeiffer household than his own, absorbing the vibrant world of entertainment.

Elias Disney, ever the enterprising and industrious figure, purchased a newspaper delivery route for *The Kansas City Star* and *Kansas City Times*, a venture that required significant dedication and hard work from his sons, Walt and Roy. The responsibility of managing this newspaper route fell largely on the young shoulders of Walt and his brother. Their daily routine was grueling; it began with waking up at 3:30 AM, long before the sun rose, to deliver newspapers across the neighborhood. This early morning routine had to be completed before they could head to school. After a full day of classes, their work was not yet done; they repeated the newspaper route in the evening, ensuring that the evening editions reached their subscribers.

This relentless schedule took a significant toll on Walt's school performance. The early mornings and late afternoons left him perpetually exhausted, and it was not uncommon for him to doze off during classes. His teachers often found him struggling to stay awake, his grades reflecting the fatigue that overshadowed his school days. Despite these challenges, Walt's dedication to his responsibilities and

---

* Vaudeville was a popular form of variety entertainment in the United States and Canada from the late 19th century until the early 1930s. It featured a series of separate, unrelated acts grouped together on a common bill. These acts could include musicians, dancers, comedians, trained animals, magicians, impersonators, acrobats, jugglers, one-act plays, athletes, lectures, minstrels, or films. Vaudeville performances were known for their broad appeal, catering to a diverse audience by offering a wide range of entertainment styles in a single show.

his willingness to support his family demonstrated a remarkable level of discipline and work ethic for someone his age. These early experiences of hard work, perseverance, and responsibility would prove invaluable in his later life, instilling qualities that would drive him through the many challenges he would face in building his entertainment empire.

It was a time of hard work and sacrifice, but also one of growth and learning. These experiences did not just build his character; they forged the foundation upon which he would build his dreams, paving the way for the creation of some of the most beloved and enduring works of entertainment the world has ever seen.

Amid all this, Walt's passion for art never waned. He managed to carve out time to nurture his creative talents, driven by an unyielding desire to improve and express himself through his drawings. Recognizing the need for formal training to enhance his skills, around 1917, when he was about sixteen years old, Walt enrolled in Saturday courses at the Kansas City Art Institute. These classes provided him with a structured environment where he could learn new techniques and receive guidance from experienced artists. The exposure to different artistic styles and the constructive feedback from instructors played a crucial role in refining his abilities.

In addition to attending the art institute, Walt also enrolled in a correspondence course in cartooning. This course allowed him to learn at his own pace and delve deeper into the world of cartoons, a medium that fascinated him immensely. The lessons from the correspondence course covered various aspects of cartooning, from character design and storytelling to the technical skills needed for animation. Walt diligently completed the assignments, often staying up late into the night to practice and perfect his craft.

These educational experiences were more than just a means to improve his drawing skills; they opened up new artistic horizons for Walt. He began to see the potential of cartoons not just as simple drawings, but as powerful tools for storytelling and communication. The combination of formal instruction and self-directed learning helped him develop a unique style that blended creativity with technical proficiency.

In 1917, Elias Disney, always on the lookout for new business opportunities, invested in the O-Zell Company, a jelly producer based in Chicago. This investment prompted the Disney family to relocate back to Chicago, marking another significant transition in young Walt's life. Returning to the bustling city from the quieter environment of Kansas City, Walt enrolled at McKinley High School. Here, he quickly became involved in the school newspaper, contributing cartoons that often reflected the patriotic fervor of the time, as World War I was at its height. These cartoons not only showcased his burgeoning talent but also his growing ability to capture and comment on contemporary issues through his art.

Simultaneously, Walt was determined to further his artistic education. Recognizing the importance of formal training, he took night classes at the Chicago Academy of Fine Arts. These classes provided him with a rigorous curriculum and access to skilled instructors who helped him refine his technique and expand his artistic repertoire. Walt immersed himself in his studies, learning the fundamentals of drawing, composition, and the principles of design. This period of intensive study was crucial in honing his skills and preparing him for the professional challenges that lay ahead.

Despite his deep engagement with art and school, Walt was also deeply affected by the ongoing war. In mid-1918, driven by a sense of duty and a desire to serve his country, he attempted to enlist in the United States Army. However, he was rejected for being underage as he was only sixteen years old – a common hurdle for many young men eager to join the war effort. Undeterred by this setback, Walt took a bold step by forging the date of birth on his birth certificate, enabling him to join the Red Cross as an ambulance driver. This decision demonstrated his determination and resourcefulness, traits that would later define his career.

Walt's experience with the Red Cross proved to be a transformative period in his life. Although he arrived in France after the Armistice had been signed, the opportunity to serve in a war-torn country broadened his worldview significantly. The sights, sounds, and stories of post-war Europe left a permanent mark on him. He witnessed the devastation and the resilience of people rebuilding their lives, experiences that would influence his later storytelling. Walt also continued to draw, using his art to document and interpret his surroundings. He decorated his ambulance with cartoons and sketches, and some of his work was published in the *Stars and Stripes*, the American military newspaper. This exposure helped him gain confidence in his abilities and introduced his work to a broader audience.

Walt's time in France also exposed him to a more liberated lifestyle. Away from his parents' strict oversight, he indulged in some partying, culminating in a lively 18th birthday party thrown by his co-workers in the ambulance corps. Despite these distractions, Walt found solace in his art, painting the sides of ambulances with cartoonish depictions of his colleagues. His creativity extended to a money-making scheme with a fellow soldier, where they transformed pristine German helmets into battle-worn war trophies, earning Walt about $300 ($5,926 in today's economy).

Upon returning to the United States, Walt felt a renewed sense of purpose. After spending some time with his parents in Chicago, he moved to Kansas City to live with his older brother Roy. In Kansas City, Walt sought to establish himself professionally. He found employment as an apprentice artist at the Pesmen-Rubin Commercial Art Studio. This position was a significant step in his career, allowing him to work on commercial illustrations for advertising, theater programs, and catalogs. The work was diverse and challenging, providing Walt with valuable experience in creating art that met commercial and promotional needs. He learned to balance creativity with the practical demands of clients, a skill that would be essential in his later ventures.

It was at Pesmen-Rubin that Walt met Ub Iwerks, a fellow artist who would become one of the most important collaborators in his career. The two young men quickly formed a strong friendship, bonded by their shared passion for art and animation. Iwerks  was an exceptionally talented draftsman, and together, they began to dream of creating their own animations. This partnership would prove to be pivotal, as Iwerks' technical skills complemented Walt's visionary ideas, laying the groundwork for their future successes.

During their time at Pesmen-Rubin, Walt and Ub began experimenting with animation, fascinated by the possibilities of bringing drawings to life. The two quickly became friends and began experimenting with animation techniques, studying the works of pioneers like Winsor McCay, Émile Cohl, and J.R. Bray, drawing inspiration from the possibilities of combining art and motion. This period of experimentation and learning was crucial, as it helped them develop the skills and knowledge needed to start their own animation studio.

As Walt continued to work at Pesmen-Rubin, he became increasingly determined to pursue his dreams of creating animated films. His experiences in Chicago and Kansas City had provided him with a solid foundation in both artistic skills and professional resilience. The discipline he had developed through his early morning newspaper routes, the artistic growth from his formal training, and the broadened perspective from his time in the Red Cross all converged to prepare him for the challenges ahead.

By 1920, Walt and Ub Iwerks decided to take a bold step toward realizing their dreams. They left Pesmen-Rubin to start their own business, a venture that would eventually evolve into the Laugh-O-Gram Studio. Although this initial foray into the world of animation was fraught with financial difficulties and setbacks, it marked the beginning of Walt Disney's journey to becoming a pioneering force in the entertainment industry.

Through the struggles and triumphs of these early years, Walt Disney's unwavering determination, innovative spirit, and passion for storytelling continued to drive him forward. His friendship with Ub Iwerks, forged during their time at Pesmen-Rubin, would prove to be one of the most fruitful collaborations in animation history. Together, they would lay the foundations for the magical world of Disney, captivating audiences around the globe and leaving an enduring legacy.

Walt Disney's journey into the world of animation began with a dream and a relentless drive to bring his creative ideas to life. In 1920, with aspirations to pursue their dreams further, Walt and his close collaborator, Ub Iwerks, left their positions at the Pesmen-Rubin Commercial Art Studio. They joined the Kansas City Slide Company, which, although financially modest, provided them with a crucial platform to refine their skills and experiment with animated content. This period was pivotal as it allowed Walt to gain valuable experience and insight into the burgeoning field of animation.

Walt's entrepreneurial spirit and growing confidence soon led him to take a bold step in his career. In 1921, he established his own company, Laugh-O-Gram Studio. This venture marked a significant milestone in Disney's journey, showcasing his determination to carve out a space in the animation industry. The studio was aptly named

"Laugh-O-Gram" to reflect the whimsical and humorous nature of the content Walt envisioned producing, aiming to bring joy and laughter to audiences.

Securing a contract with local dentist Thomas B. McCrum was a critical move for Disney. This contract involved producing short animated advertisements, which provided crucial financial support for the fledgling studio. These advertisements not only helped sustain the business but also offered Walt an opportunity to explore and experiment with the medium of animation more freely. The work done during this period laid the foundation for Disney's future successes, allowing him to hone his storytelling and technical skills.

Laugh-O-Gram Studio, located in a small office in Kansas City, was modest in its beginnings. Despite its humble setup, it was a starting point where Walt could bring his creative visions to life. The studio became a hub of innovation and creativity, attracting a group of talented artists and animators who shared Walt's passion and drive. This collective effort led to the creation of several short films, including adaptations of fairy tales and original stories, which began to attract local attention.

One of the first major projects undertaken by Laugh-O-Gram Studio was a series of modernized fairy tales. These shorts, inspired by classic stories, were given a contemporary twist to appeal to modern audiences. The series included titles like *Little Red Riding Hood*, *The Four Musicians of Bremen*, and *Puss in Boots*. Each of these projects was unique in its approach, showcasing Walt Disney's talent for blending traditional narratives with modern sensibilities, making them both accessible and entertaining to viewers of the time.

*Little Red Riding Hood* was one of the earliest fairy tales adapted by Laugh-O-Gram. In Walt's version, the story retained its core elements but included humorous twists and contemporary references. The classic tale of a young girl who encounters a cunning wolf on her way to visit her grandmother was reimagined with new characters and settings that resonated with the 1920s audience. The wolf, for example, was depicted with exaggerated, comical features, adding a layer of humor that softened the darker aspects of the original tale.

This approach made the story more engaging and enjoyable for children and adults alike, demonstrating Walt's ability to innovate while respecting the source material.

Another significant project was *The Four Musicians of Bremen*. This story, based on the Brothers Grimm fairy tale, follows four aging animals – a donkey, a dog, a cat, and a rooster – who set out to become musicians in the town of Bremen after their respective owners decide they are no longer useful. Walt's adaptation injected new life into this story by giving the animals distinct personalities and humorous quirks. The animation featured lively musical sequences and comedic interactions, emphasizing teamwork and the joy of pursuing one's dreams despite obstacles. This project highlighted Walt's knack for character development and his ability to infuse classic stories with vibrant, entertaining elements.

*Puss in Boots* was another standout in the series. This tale, also derived from a classic fairy tale, tells the story of a clever cat who uses trickery and cunning to gain wealth and power for his master. Walt's version of *Puss in Boots* added a playful and adventurous tone to the narrative. The cat, with his signature boots and hat, was portrayed as a charismatic and witty character who outsmarted various adversaries. The animation was rich with imaginative scenarios and clever visual gags, showcasing Walt's creativity and his team's animation skills. This project further solidified Walt's reputation for breathing new life into well-known stories, making them appealing to a modern audience.

The production process at Laugh-O-Gram was grueling and required immense dedication from Walt and his small team of animators. Animation in those days was a labor-intensive process, with each frame painstakingly drawn by hand. The team worked long hours to create the fluid motion and expressive characters that defined their work. Walt and Ub Iwerks, along with other animators, often worked late into the night, driven by their passion for animation and storytelling. The studio, though modest in resources, was a hive of creativity and innovation.

To create these animated shorts, the team used a technique called "cutout animation." This method involved creating characters and

elements out of paper or cardboard, which were then manipulated frame by frame to simulate movement. While this technique was less expensive and time-consuming than traditional cel animation, which involves hand-drawing each frame on transparent celluloid sheets, it still required meticulous attention to detail and precise coordination. The animators had to ensure that each movement was smooth and natural, which meant hours of painstaking work for just a few seconds of film.

Despite the challenges, the team at Laugh-O-Gram Studio was driven by a shared vision of pushing the boundaries of animation. They experimented with various techniques to improve the quality of their work, such as combining live-action footage with animation, a concept that Walt would revisit later in his career. This period of experimentation and innovation was crucial in developing the skills and knowledge needed to create more sophisticated animations in the future.

In an effort to expand their reach and attract a broader audience, Walt decided to produce a pilot film titled *Alice's Wonderland*. This innovative film combined live-action with animation, starring a young actress named Virginia Davis as Alice. In the film, Alice interacts with animated characters in a whimsical world, blending the real and the fantastical in a way that was groundbreaking for its time. *Alice's Wonderland* was a precursor to the famous Alice Comedies series that Walt would later develop, showcasing his ability to think outside the box and create content that was both unique and captivating.

The concept of *Alice's Wonderland* was inspired by the Lewis Carroll classic, but Walt's version took significant creative liberties. In this film, Alice, played by Virginia Davis, dreams of visiting an animated wonderland. She encounters a variety of whimsical characters and scenarios, blending the innocence and curiosity of childhood with the limitless possibilities of animation. The film featured innovative techniques, such as integrating live-action footage with animated backgrounds and characters, which added a new dimension to the storytelling. This project demonstrated Walt's visionary thinking and his willingness to explore new frontiers in animation.

Despite the creative success of *Alice's Wonderland* and the fairy tale series, financial backing remained difficult to find. The high costs of producing animated shorts and the limited revenue from contracts and advertisements placed immense pressure on Laugh-O-Gram Studio. Walt faced constant financial struggles, often going without pay to ensure his employees received their wages. His dedication to his team and his unwavering belief in the potential of animation kept him going, even as the studio's financial situation grew increasingly dire.

By 1923, the financial challenges had reached a breaking point. Unable to secure enough contracts to keep the studio afloat, Laugh-O-Gram Studio declared bankruptcy. This was a significant setback for Walt, leaving him disillusioned and deeply in debt. However, even in the face of adversity, his determination never wavered. The experiences and lessons he gained at Laugh-O-Gram were invaluable. He had learned the intricacies of animation production, the challenges of managing a business, and the importance of innovation and storytelling. These lessons would serve him well in his future ventures.

After the closure of Laugh-O-Gram Studio, Walt decided to move to Hollywood to seek new opportunities. He believed that the burgeoning film industry in California offered better prospects for his talents and ambitions. With little money but a heart full of dreams, Walt set out for Hollywood in the summer of 1923, carrying with him the film reel of *Alice's Wonderland*. Upon arriving in Hollywood, Walt teamed up with his brother Roy, who was recovering from tuberculosis. Roy's business acumen and financial support complemented Walt's creative vision, and together they formed the Disney Brothers Studio.

The legacy of Laugh-O-Gram Studio was significant, despite its ultimate failure. It was here that Walt Disney honed his skills as an animator and storyteller. The studio's innovative approach to modernizing fairy tales and experimenting with live-action/animation combinations laid the groundwork for Disney's later successes. Moreover, the relationships and partnerships formed during this period were crucial. Ub Iwerks, who had been a key collaborator at Laugh-O-Gram, followed Walt to Hollywood and continued to play a vital role in the development of Disney's early animated works. Their partnership would lead to the creation of iconic characters and groundbreaking animation techniques.

The challenges and failures experienced at Laugh-O-Gram Studio taught Walt several important lessons. He learned the necessity of financial management and the importance of securing reliable funding for creative projects. The experience also underscored the need for innovation and quality in entertainment, principles that would guide him throughout his career. Walt's persistence and resilience in the face of adversity were perhaps the most critical lessons of all. Despite the collapse of his first venture, he remained undeterred in his pursuit of his dreams. This unwavering determination became a defining characteristic of Walt Disney's career, driving him to continually push the boundaries of animation and storytelling.

The end of Laugh-O-Gram Studio marked a turning point in Walt Disney's life. It was the end of one chapter but the beginning of another, more successful phase. The move to Hollywood and the formation of the Disney Brothers Studio set the stage for the creation of Mickey Mouse and the establishment of Walt Disney as a pioneering figure in animation. The lessons learned and the experiences gained during the Laugh-O-Gram years were instrumental in shaping Walt's approach to animation and business. He carried forward the innovative spirit and creative ambition that had defined Laugh-O-Gram, but with a renewed focus on financial stability and strategic growth.

# The Birth of Mickey Mouse

When Disney moved to Hollywood in 1923, the first major break came when they secured a distribution deal with Margaret J. Winkler, a New York film distributor. Winkler was losing the rights to the popular *Out of the Inkwell* and *Felix the Cat* cartoons and needed a new series. In October 1923, she signed a contract with the Disney brothers for six Alice Comedies, with an option for two further series of six episodes each. The Disney brothers persuaded Virginia Davis and her family to relocate to Hollywood, with Davis on contract at $100 a month to continue her role as Alice, which would be equivalent to approximately $1,733 in today's time.

By July 1924, Disney also hired Ub Iwerks, persuading him to relocate to Hollywood from Kansas City. Iwerks' incredible animation skills were integral to the success of the studio. Together, they continued producing the Alice Comedies, which combined live-action footage of

Davis with animated characters. The series gained moderate success, and by 1926, the Disney Brothers Studio was thriving enough to establish its first official studio at 2725 Hyperion Avenue. This location would become a historic site for Disney's burgeoning empire, although it was demolished in 1940.

While Disney was juggling between creating the Alice comedy series, his personal life was blooming with newfound love. In early 1925, Disney hired an ink artist named Lillian Bounds, who quickly became an integral part of his life. Born on February 15, 1899, in Spalding, Idaho, Lillian Bounds grew up in Lapwai, Idaho, on the Nez Perce Indian Reservation, where her father worked as a blacksmith and federal marshal. In 1923, she had moved to Los Angeles to secure a job which she ended up getting at Disney's company.

They married in July of that same year, holding the ceremony at her brother's house in Lewiston, Idaho, her hometown. Their marriage was a happy ordeal. However, breaking the gender roles of that time Lillian was not meek. She never accepted her husband's status without questioning, and always proved to be an equal partner to him. Even though she was a keen artist, Lillian was also not interested in the 'Hollywood scene,' often preferring taking care of the household and Disney. The Disney family recalls that Walt never entered the house without hugging and kissing Lillian and spoke of her with pride. He respected her authority on household matters, always gave her the window seat on airplanes, and let her choose their hotel rooms.

Meanwhile in Walt's professional life, as the Alice series continued, Margaret J. Winkler's role in its distribution was taken over by her husband, Charles Mintz. Although the relationship between Disney and Mintz was sometimes strained, they managed to keep the series running until July 1927. By this time, Walt Disney had grown tired of the mixed-format approach of the Alice Comedies and wanted to transition to all-animation films. Mintz, seeing the potential in

Disney's vision, requested new material to distribute through Universal Pictures.

This led to the creation of Oswald the Lucky Rabbit, a character Disney wanted to be "peppy, alert, saucy and venturesome, keeping him also neat and trim." Oswald was designed to be a cheerful, adventurous character who could easily endear himself to audiences. He was sleek and simple in design, allowing for a range of expressive animations that brought out his playful personality. Oswald's large eyes, floppy ears, and lively movements quickly made him a favorite among viewers, and he debuted in 1927 to considerable success.

The Oswald series was a breakthrough for Disney, marking his first significant success in the world of animation. The character's adventures were well-received, and the Oswald shorts were distributed widely, enhancing Disney's reputation as a talented animator and storyteller. This success, however, was not to last. In February 1928, as Disney sought to negotiate a larger fee for producing the Oswald series, he encountered a significant setback that would test his resolve and ultimately change the course of his career.

During the negotiations, Charles Mintz, who was distributing the Oswald cartoons through Universal Pictures, not only refused Disney's request for a higher fee but also presented a stark ultimatum. Mintz proposed a reduction in the payments for the cartoons, arguing that the series was expensive to produce. Disney, who had invested heavily in the quality and creativity of his animations, was taken aback by this proposal. The situation quickly escalated when Disney discovered that Mintz had been working behind the scenes to undermine him.

Mintz had secretly persuaded many of Disney's key animators to leave Disney Brothers Studio and work directly for him. Among those who agreed to defect were some of Disney's most talented and essential staff, including Hugh Harman, Rudolf Ising, Carman Maxwell, and Friz Freleng. These artists had been integral to the success of the

Oswald series, and their departure was a significant blow to Disney. The betrayal by his trusted team members was not only a professional setback but also a personal disappointment for Disney, who had always strived to foster a collaborative and creative environment at his studio.

Adding to Disney's troubles, he discovered that Universal Pictures owned the intellectual property rights to Oswald the Lucky Rabbit. This meant that even if Disney refused Mintz's demands, he could not take Oswald with him. Mintz used this leverage to threaten Disney, stating that if Disney did not accept the reduced payments, he would establish his own studio and continue producing the Oswald series without him. This ultimatum left Disney with little room to maneuver. Faced with the loss of his staff and his beloved character, Disney had to make a crucial decision.

Determined not to compromise on his principles or the quality of his work, Disney declined Mintz's ultimatum. This decision came at a great cost, as he lost most of his animation staff and the rights to Oswald. However, one loyal animator chose to remain with Disney: Ub Iwerks. Iwerks' decision to stay was a testament to his belief in Disney's vision and his dedication to their partnership. Together, they faced the daunting task of rebuilding from the ground up.

This challenging period was a turning point for Walt Disney. The loss of Oswald and the betrayal by his staff were significant blows, but they also ignited a spark of determination and creativity in Disney. He realized the importance of retaining creative control over his work and the need to create a character that he fully owned.

This betrayal and the loss of Oswald were a major blow to Walt Disney, but it also set the stage for one of the most significant developments in animation history: the birth of Mickey Mouse in 1928. Determined to create a new character that he owned outright, Disney and Iwerks went back to the drawing board. Inspired by a pet mouse Walt had while working at Laugh-O-Gram Studio, they began to develop a new character. Disney's original choice for the character's name was Mortimer Mouse, but his wife Lillian found it too overbearing and suggested the name Mickey instead. Iwerks revised

Disney's first few sketches, making the character simpler and easier to animate.

Mickey Mouse was born out of necessity and a desire for creative control. Walt Disney, who had begun to distance himself from the animation process, provided Mickey's voice until 1947. An employee at Disney once remarked, "Ub designed Mickey's physical appearance, but Walt gave him his soul." This collaboration between Walt Disney and Ub Iwerks was crucial in creating a character that would resonate deeply with audiences and stand the test of time.

Mickey Mouse made his first appearance in a test screening of the short *Plane Crazy* in May 1928. Although it failed to find a distributor, it marked the beginning of something extraordinary. The second short, *The Gallopin' Gaucho*, also did not succeed in securing a distributor. It wasn't until Disney introduced synchronized sound in the third short, *Steamboat Willie*, that Mickey Mouse would find his place in history.

The success of *The Jazz Singer* in 1927, the first film with synchronized sound, was a revelation to Walt Disney. He realized that sound had the potential to revolutionize the animation industry and elevate the audience's experience. Inspired by this groundbreaking achievement, Disney was determined to incorporate synchronized sound into his own animations. This vision culminated in the creation of *Steamboat Willie*, which premiered on November 18, 1928, and became an immediate sensation.

*Steamboat Willie* was the first cartoon to successfully synchronize sound with animation, marking a groundbreaking achievement in the industry. The short featured Mickey Mouse as a mischievous deckhand on a riverboat, engaging in a series of  playful antics with various characters. Minnie Mouse made her debut alongside Mickey, adding to the charm and appeal of the film. The creation of Minnie Mouse was not only a stroke of creative genius but also deeply personal for Walt Disney. Minnie was inspired by Lillian

Disney, Walt's beloved wife. Lillian's playful spirit, kindness, and supportive nature were all qualities that Walt admired and sought to embody in Minnie. This personal connection added an extra layer of charm and relatability to Minnie, making her a beloved character from the start. Additionally, the use of sound brought a new level of engagement and excitement to the animation, as audiences could hear the synchronized sounds of whistles, music, and character interactions for the first time. The innovative integration of sound and visuals made *Steamboat Willie* a landmark in film history.

To achieve the synchronization, Walt Disney knew he needed to employ cutting-edge technology. He signed a contract with former Universal Pictures executive Pat Powers, who provided access to the "Powers Cinephone" recording system. This system allowed Disney to synchronize the audio track with the animated film precisely. The intricate process involved coordinating every sound effect and piece of dialogue to match the animation, ensuring that the final product was seamless and immersive.

Cinephone quickly became the new distributor for Disney's early sound cartoons, and the success of *Steamboat Willie* propelled Mickey Mouse into stardom. The character's expressive movements and synchronized sounds captivated audiences, establishing Mickey as a cultural icon. Walt Disney's decision to embrace sound technology demonstrated his visionary approach and willingness to take risks to push the boundaries of what was possible in animation.

Walt Disney's creative genius was not limited to his technical innovations. His ability to infuse his characters with personality and charm played a crucial role in Mickey Mouse's success. Disney himself brought the character to life with his distinctive vocal performance. This personal touch added depth to Mickey's character, making him relatable and endearing to audiences. Disney's attention to detail and commitment to quality were evident in every aspect of *Steamboat Willie*, from the animation to the sound design.

The immediate sensation of *Steamboat Willie* also showcased Disney's exceptional storytelling abilities. The short's plot was simple yet engaging, featuring Mickey's humorous and clever attempts to navigate his duties on the riverboat while entertaining the audience with his antics. The introduction of synchronized sound enhanced the storytelling, allowing for more dynamic and entertaining scenes that captivated viewers.

To improve the quality of the music in his cartoons, Disney hired professional composer and arranger Carl Stalling. Stalling suggested the idea of using music to drive the narrative in animations, leading to the creation of the Silly Symphony series. The first in the series, *The Skeleton Dance (1929)*, was drawn and animated entirely by Iwerks. This innovative approach used music as a core element of storytelling, setting a new standard for animated films.

Despite the phenomenal success of Mickey Mouse and the Silly Symphonies, Walt Disney and his brother Roy felt increasingly frustrated with their financial arrangement with Pat Powers. Although their cartoons were immensely popular, the Disney brothers believed they were not receiving their fair share of the profits. This growing dissatisfaction led Walt Disney to explore ways to reduce production costs while maintaining the high quality of their animations.

In 1930, Walt Disney took a significant step toward streamlining the animation process. He encouraged Ub Iwerks, his trusted collaborator and one of the most talented animators in the industry, to adopt a more efficient technique. Instead of drawing every single frame by hand, which was a time-consuming and labor-intensive process, Disney suggested focusing on key poses. These key poses would capture the essential movements and expressions of the characters, while assistants, known as inbetweeners, would fill in the intermediate frames. This method, known as keyframe animation, allowed for faster production without compromising the fluidity and quality of the animation. It was a revolutionary approach that would later become a standard practice in the animation industry.

While Disney was implementing these changes to improve efficiency, he also approached Pat Powers to renegotiate their financial terms. Given the success of Mickey Mouse and the Silly Symphonies, Disney believed it was fair to request an increase in payments for the cartoons. However, Powers had different plans. Instead of agreeing to

Disney's demands, Powers refused the request outright. Furthermore, he had been quietly working behind the scenes to undermine Disney's studio.

In a shocking turn of events, Powers managed to lure Ub Iwerks away from Disney Brothers Studio. He offered Iwerks a lucrative contract and the opportunity to head his own studio. This was a devastating blow to Walt Disney, as Iwerks was not only a close friend but also the creative genius behind much of the studio's success. Iwerks had been instrumental in the creation and development of Mickey Mouse, and his departure left a significant void in the studio's talent pool.

The loss of Iwerks sent shockwaves through the Disney Studio. Carl Stalling, the talented composer who had worked closely with Disney on the Silly Symphonies, was particularly concerned about the future of the studio. Stalling believed that without Iwerks, the Disney Studio would struggle to maintain its creative edge and high production standards. Consequently, Stalling decided to resign shortly after Iwerks left, fearing that the studio might not survive the loss of such a pivotal figure.

Walt Disney found himself at a critical juncture. The betrayal by Pat Powers and the departure of key personnel could have spelled disaster for the studio. However, Disney's resilience and determination came to the forefront. His ability to adapt and his relentless pursuit of excellence soon paid off. He began to recruit new talent, bringing in fresh perspectives and ideas. The new animators, although initially inexperienced, quickly learned the ropes under Disney's guidance. Walt's leadership and vision inspired his team to push the boundaries of what was possible in animation.

One of Disney's key hires during this period was a young animator named Fred Moore, whose distinctive style and innovative techniques would later become synonymous with the Disney brand. Moore's contributions helped to refine the look of Disney's characters, making them more appealing and expressive. This new wave of talent injected a renewed sense of energy and creativity into the studio.

This tumultuous period took a toll on Walt Disney, leading to a nervous breakdown in October 1931, which he attributed to overwork and the stress caused by Powers' machinations. To recover, Walt and his wife Lillian took an extended holiday to Cuba and a cruise to Panama. This break allowed Disney to regain his strength and clarity, coming back more determined than ever to push forward.

With the loss of Powers as a distributor, Disney Studios signed a contract with Columbia Pictures to distribute the Mickey Mouse cartoons. The popularity of Mickey Mouse continued to grow, both domestically and internationally. Disney and his crew also introduced new cartoon stars like Pluto in 1930, Goofy in 1932, and Donald Duck in 1934. These characters expanded the Disney universe and became beloved icons in their own right.

Always keen to embrace new technology, Disney was encouraged by his new contract with United Artists to experiment further. In 1932, he produced *Flowers and Trees*, the first animated film in full-color three-strip Technicolor. This innovative use of color brought a new vibrancy to animations and set a new industry standard.

The three-strip Technicolor process was a groundbreaking technique in the world of filmmaking. It involved using a special camera that simultaneously exposed three separate strips of black-and-white film, each through a different colored filter (red, green, and blue). These three strips were then processed and combined to create a full-color image. This method was far superior to earlier two-color processes, providing a much broader and more realistic color palette.

Disney's use of the three-strip Technicolor process allowed *Flowers and Trees* to dazzle audiences with its lush, vibrant hues and rich detail, something previously unseen in animated films. Recognizing the competitive advantage this technology offered, Disney negotiated a deal that gave him the exclusive right to use the three-strip process until August 31, 1935. This exclusivity ensured that Disney's films were visually distinct from those of his competitors, further solidifying his position as a leader and innovator in the animation industry.

*Flowers and Trees* was a hit with audiences and won the inaugural Academy Award for Best Short Subject (Cartoon) at the 1932 ceremony. Disney was also nominated for another film in that category, *Mickey's Orphans*, and received an Honorary Award for the creation of Mickey Mouse. These accolades affirmed Disney's position as a leading figure in the animation industry.

In 1933, Disney produced *The Three Little Pigs*, a film that media historian Adrian Danks described as "the most successful short animation of all time." The film's catchy song *Who's Afraid of the Big Bad Wolf?* became a cultural phenomenon, symbolizing  resilience during the Great Depression. The Great Depression, which began with the stock market crash of 1929 and lasted through most of the 1930s, was a severe worldwide economic downturn. It led to widespread unemployment, poverty, and a significant decline in economic activity. Millions of people lost their jobs, homes, and savings, facing unprecedented hardships and uncertainty. In this context, *Who's Afraid of the Big Bad Wolf?* resonated deeply with audiences. The song, featured in Disney's 1933 animated short *The Three Little Pigs*, provided a sense of hope and defiance. Its cheerful melody and lyrics about outsmarting and overcoming a menacing threat echoed the public's desire for resilience and optimism in the face of economic adversity. The song became an anthem of sorts, uplifting spirits and reminding people of their ability to endure and prevail despite difficult times.

Moreover, *The Three Little Pigs* won Disney another Academy Award in the Short Subject (Cartoon) category. Its success led to a significant expansion of the studio's staff, which numbered nearly 200 by the end of the year.

Recognizing the importance of storytelling, Disney invested in a dedicated story department, separate from the animators. This department, staffed with storyboard artists, meticulously detailed the plots of Disney's films. This focus on narrative structure ensured that Disney's animations were not only visually appealing but also emotionally engaging and coherent stories.

The birth of Mickey Mouse marked a turning point in Walt Disney's career. From the creation of Oswald the Lucky Rabbit to the invention of Mickey Mouse, Disney's journey was filled with challenges, betrayals, and breakthroughs. The success of *Steamboat Willie* and the subsequent popularity of Mickey Mouse solidified Disney's position in the entertainment industry. Mickey's evolution from a simple sketch to a cultural icon was a testament to Disney's vision and perseverance.

While Disney was experiencing remarkable professional success, his family life was also evolving and growing richer through these years. Disney and his wife welcomed their first daughter, Diane, in December 1933. The arrival of their second daughter, Sharon, who was adopted in December 1936 just six weeks after her birth, brought even more joy. Within the Disney family, Sharon's adoption was openly acknowledged, but both Walt and Lillian were protective of this information. They valued privacy and became irritated if outsiders raised the topic.

The Disney family was deeply aware of the potential dangers that public exposure could bring. The infamous Lindbergh kidnapping[*] in 1932 had left a lasting impression on many American families, and the Disneys were no exception. Determined to shield their daughters from similar risks, Walt and Lillian took significant measures to keep Diane and Sharon out of the public eye. They ensured that their daughters

---

[*] The Lindbergh kidnapping refers to the abduction and subsequent murder of Charles Lindbergh Jr., the 20-month-old son of famous aviator Charles Lindbergh and his wife, Anne Morrow Lindbergh. The crime occurred on the evening of March 1, 1932, when the child was taken from his crib in the Lindbergh family home in Hopewell, New Jersey. A ransom note demanding $50,000 was left at the scene.

were rarely photographed by the press, preserving their privacy with great care. Walt went to great lengths to protect his daughters, instilling a sense of security and normalcy in their lives despite his public prominence.

In an anecdote, Diane shared that Walt patiently taught both of his daughters how to ride horses, sparking a lifelong love for the animals. When they were young, the girls even declared that they would marry horses when they grew up. Diane Disney Miller fondly remembered these moments: her father setting her on the horse, leading her around with the lead rope, and spending hours helping her overcome her fear of horses. Walt was always taking pictures, capturing countless images of Diane showing off on the horse at about five years old, making faces and having fun. His dedication and enthusiasm not only helped Diane conquer her fears but also created cherished memories immortalized in his many photographs.

The Disneys' dedication to their daughters' privacy extended beyond merely avoiding the press. They structured their lives to provide a stable and nurturing environment for Diane and Sharon. Lillian, who had little interest in films or the Hollywood social scene, after growing up found fulfillment in managing the household and supporting her husband. She created a home that was a sanctuary away from Walt's demanding career, where their children could grow up away from the spotlight.

Walt Disney's professional success and his dedication to his family were tightly intertwined. The support and stability provided by Lillian and the joy brought by their daughters fueled his creativity and ambition. His ability to compartmentalize and balance his public and private lives was a testament to his character and the values he held dear. As his empire grew, so did his commitment to maintaining the privacy and security of his loved ones, ensuring that his family remained grounded and protected amidst the ever-increasing demands of his career.

The Disneys' careful management of their private lives allowed Walt to focus on his visionary projects, knowing that his family was safe and secure. This balance between personal and professional life was crucial as he embarked on one of his most ambitious projects: the creation of the first feature-length animated film, *Snow White and the Seven Dwarfs*. The stability of his family life provided a strong foundation that enabled Walt to take bold creative risks, ultimately leading to groundbreaking achievements in the world of animation.

By 1934, Walt Disney had grown increasingly dissatisfied with the limitations of producing cartoon shorts. His ambition and vision for animation went far beyond the constraints of short films, and he believed that a feature-length cartoon would not only push the boundaries of the medium but also prove to be more profitable. This ambitious idea led to the inception of *Snow White and the Seven Dwarfs*, a project that would eventually become a landmark in cinematic history.

The decision to create a feature-length animated film was bold and risky. The industry had never seen anything like it, and many in Hollywood were skeptical. When news of the project leaked out, industry insiders were quick to call it "Disney's Folly," predicting that it would bankrupt the studio. Despite the skeptics, Walt Disney was unwavering in his determination. He believed in the power of storytelling through animation and was confident that audiences would embrace a full-length animated feature if it was done with quality and care.

The production of *Snow White and the Seven Dwarfs* began in 1934 and spanned over four years. The project was an enormous undertaking, requiring out-of-the-ordinary resources and innovation. Disney's commitment to quality led him to invest heavily in training and development for his animators. He sent his team to the Chouinard Art Institute to take courses that would enhance their skills, particularly in capturing realistic movements. Additionally, Disney brought live animals into the studio and hired actors to perform scenes, allowing animators to study and replicate the nuances of realistic motion in their drawings.

One of the key technical advancements developed during the production was the multiplane camera. This device allowed drawings on pieces of glass to be set at various distances from the camera, creating an illusion of depth. The glass plates could be moved independently to simulate the changing perspectives as a camera passed through a scene. The multiplane camera was first used in the Silly Symphony short *The Old Mill* in 1937, which won the Academy Award for Animated Short Film due to its impressive visual power. Recognizing the potential of this new technique, Disney ordered some scenes in *Snow White* to be re-drawn to incorporate the multiplane effects, even though the film was largely finished by that time.

As production progressed, the costs began to mount. Originally budgeted at $250,000, the final cost of *Snow White and the Seven Dwarfs* ballooned to $1.5 million, six times over budget. Adjusted for inflation, this would be approximately $31.2 million in today's money. The financial strain was significant, and Disney had to mortgage his house to help finance the film. Despite these pressures, Disney remained focused on his vision, ensuring that every aspect of the film met his high standards.

The production of *Snow White and the Seven Dwarfs* was a monumental effort that required meticulous planning, creative ingenuity, and unwavering perseverance. Disney's dedication to the project was evident in every frame of the film. He was involved in all aspects of production, from story development to final animation. His ability to inspire and lead his team was a key factor in overcoming the numerous challenges that arose during the production.

Disney's approach to character development in *Snow White* was particularly groundbreaking. He wanted each of the seven dwarfs to have distinct personalities, a concept that required careful thought and detailed animation. The dwarfs – Doc, Grumpy, Happy, Sleepy, Bashful, Sneezy, and Dopey – were each given unique traits and behaviors that made them memorable and endearing to audiences. This focus on character individuality was a significant departure from the more generic animated characters of the past and set a new standard for future animations.

*Snow White and the Seven Dwarfs* premiered on December 21, 1937, at the Carthay Circle Theatre in Los Angeles. The premiere was a star-studded event, attended by Hollywood's elite, including Charlie Chaplin and Shirley Temple. As the film began, the audience was transported into a richly detailed and enchanting world, unlike anything they had seen before. The film received a standing ovation, and critics were unanimous in their praise. *Snow White* was hailed as a groundbreaking achievement in animation and a testament to Walt Disney's visionary genius.

The success of *Snow White and the Seven Dwarfs* was immediate and overwhelming. The film captivated audiences with its groundbreaking animation, enchanting story, and memorable characters. Premiering in December 1937, *Snow White* quickly became the most successful motion picture of 1938. By May 1939, it had grossed an astounding $6.5 million (approximately $87 million in today's money considering inflation), making it the highest-grossing sound film at that time. This financial triumph was unprecedented for an animated feature and demonstrated the immense potential of animation as a medium.

Beyond its financial success, *Snow White* had a profound cultural impact. It solidified animation as a legitimate and respected art form, capable of delivering complex narratives and eliciting deep emotional responses from audiences. Prior to *Snow White*, animation was largely viewed as a novelty or a medium for short, humorous cartoons. The success of this feature-length film changed that perception, showcasing the power of animation to tell compelling, full-length stories that could rival live-action films in their depth and artistry.

Walt Disney's achievement with *Snow White* was widely recognized within the film industry. In 1939, Disney was awarded an honorary Academy Award for the film. The award was a unique and fitting tribute: it consisted of one full-sized Oscar statuette and  of one full-sized Oscar statuette and seven miniature ones, presented by the child star Shirley Temple. This gesture symbolized the film's blend of grandeur and charm, and it honored Disney's pioneering work in animation.

The triumph of *Snow White and the Seven Dwarfs* marked the beginning of what is often referred to as the "Golden Age of Animation" for the Walt Disney Studio. This period, spanning the late 1930s to the early 1940s, was characterized by a series of innovative and influential animated films that continued to push the boundaries of the medium. The success of *Snow White* provided Disney with the financial resources and the confidence to invest in new and ambitious projects. With the success of *Snow White*, Disney was able to invest in new projects, leading to the production of *Pinocchio* and *Fantasia*.

Production on *Pinocchio* began in early 1938, followed by *Fantasia* in November of the same year. Both films were released in 1940, showcasing Disney's continued commitment to innovation and storytelling. *Pinocchio* featured novel advancements in animation techniques, including realistic character movements and intricate special effects. The film's story of a wooden puppet's quest to become a real boy resonated with audiences, further establishing Disney's reputation for creating emotionally compelling narratives.

*Fantasia*, on the other hand, was an ambitious and experimental project that combined classical music with imaginative and abstract animation. The film was designed as a series of eight animated segments set to pieces of classical music conducted by Leopold

Stokowski. *Fantasia* was unlike any other film at the time, offering a unique and immersive audiovisual experience. Despite its artistic achievements and innovative use of stereophonic sound, *Fantasia* did not perform well at the box office initially, partly due to the onset of World War II, which affected international revenues.

The financial performance of *Pinocchio* and *Fantasia* was disappointing, and the studio had to face significant losses on both pictures. By the end of February 1941, the Disney Studio was deeply in debt. Despite the setbacks, Walt Disney remained committed to his vision and continued to explore new ways to innovate and captivate audiences.

As Walt Disney looked to the future, the lessons learned from the production of *Snow White* and the subsequent feature films would guide the studio's continued evolution. The "Golden Age of Animation" that followed was characterized by a series of iconic films that built on the foundations laid by *Snow White*, each pushing the boundaries of what was possible in the medium.

The financial strain from the underperformance of *Pinocchio* and *Fantasia*, coupled with the ongoing war, led to significant challenges for the Disney Studio in the early 1940s. These two ambitious projects had not brought in the expected revenue, and the studio was facing mounting debts. The financial pressure was intense, and something drastic had to be done to stabilize the company. In response, Walt Disney and his brother Roy initiated the company's first public stock offering in 1940, a bold move aimed at raising much-needed capital. This decision marked a significant shift for the company, as it opened up ownership to public investors for the first time.

Alongside the stock offering, the Disney brothers also implemented heavy salary cuts across the board. These drastic measures were necessary to keep the studio afloat but were deeply unpopular among the staff. The combination of salary reductions and the high demands placed on the animators created a tense atmosphere within the studio. Walt Disney, known for his perfectionism and sometimes high-handed approach, exacerbated the situation with his insensitivity toward the growing discontent among his employees.

The tension reached a breaking point in 1941, leading to a five-week animators' strike. The strike was a significant and tumultuous event in the history of the Disney Studio. It highlighted the growing rift between Walt Disney and his staff, many of whom felt undervalued and overworked. The strike began on May 29, 1941, led by the Screen Cartoonists Guild*, which demanded better wages, improved working conditions, and recognition of their union.

The strike quickly gained momentum, with picket lines forming outside the studio and production grinding to a halt. The colorful picket signs and the presence of many well-known animators brought considerable media attention to the strike. The dispute not only disrupted the production schedule but also damaged the once-strong camaraderie within the studio. Walt Disney took the strike personally, feeling betrayed by his employees. His reaction further strained relationships, and several animators left the studio, either in protest or because they were dismissed.

During the strike, Walt Disney accepted an offer from the Office of the Coordinator of Inter-American Affairs to make a goodwill trip to South America. This trip was part of the U.S. government's Good Neighbor Policy, aimed at strengthening ties with Latin American countries during World War II. Disney's absence during the resolution of the strike allowed him to avoid directly dealing with the unfavorable settlement terms that the federal mediator from the National Labor Relations Board eventually imposed. By not being present, Disney distanced himself from the negotiations and the

---

* The Screen Cartoonists Guild, officially known as the Motion Picture Screen Cartoonists Guild, was a labor union established to represent the interests of animators, artists, and other workers in the animation industry. Founded in 1938, the guild aimed to improve working conditions, secure fair wages, and provide benefits for its members. It emerged during a period when labor movements were gaining momentum in various industries, including Hollywood.

resulting compromises, thus shielding himself from immediate backlash and criticism associated with the resolution. This strategic avoidance meant that Disney did not have to personally confront the dissatisfaction of the workers or the demands of the federal mediator, which may have helped him maintain a more neutral or detached public image during the conflict.

While Disney was away, the strike was eventually settled, but the resolution left a lasting impact on the studio. The animators won several of their demands, including better pay and recognition of their union, but the strike had permanently altered the dynamics within the studio. Walt's relationship with many of his employees was strained, and the sense of a close-knit, family-like atmosphere was damaged.

The strike also temporarily interrupted the production of *Dumbo*, which was already in the works. In response to the financial constraints and the disruptions caused by the strike, Disney decided to produce *Dumbo* in a simple and inexpensive manner. Unlike the lavish productions of *Pinocchio* and *Fantasia*, *Dumbo* was created with a more modest budget and a straightforward narrative. This approach proved to be a wise decision under the circumstances.

*Dumbo* was released in October 1941 and received a positive reaction from both audiences and critics. The story of the little elephant with oversized ears who learns to fly resonated with viewers, offering a message of hope and resilience. The film's simplicity and emotional depth captured the hearts of many, and it became a commercial success. The positive reception of *Dumbo* provided a much-needed boost for the Disney Studio during a challenging time.

Despite the success of *Dumbo*, the financial and emotional toll of the strike was significant. Several talented animators had left the studio, taking their skills and experience with them. The strike underscored the need for better management practices and highlighted the importance of maintaining positive relationships with employees. For Walt Disney, the strike was a painful but valuable lesson in leadership and the complexities of running a growing business.

Shortly after *Dumbo's* release, the United States entered World War II. In response, Disney formed the Walt Disney Training Films Unit to produce instructional films for the military. These films included titles like *Four Methods of Flush Riveting* and *Aircraft Production Methods*, which were designed to educate soldiers and factory workers on crucial techniques and processes needed for the war effort. These films were practical and technical, featuring detailed animations that broke down complex tasks into understandable steps, thereby enhancing training efficiency.

Disney's engagement with the war effort didn't stop at training films. He met with Secretary of the Treasury, Henry Morgenthau Jr., and agreed to produce a series of short Donald Duck cartoons to promote war bonds. These cartoons, such as *The New Spirit* and *The Spirit of '43*, featured the beloved character in patriotic roles, encouraging American citizens to financially support the war effort. The relatable and humorous nature of Donald Duck made these messages more accessible and appealing to the general public.

Additionally, Disney produced several propaganda films, including the notable *Der Fuehrer's Face*, which satirized Nazi Germany and its leader, Adolf Hitler. This film used humor and absurdity to ridicule the oppressive regime, and it was well-received, earning an Academy Award for Best Animated Short Film. Another significant production was the 1943 feature film *Victory Through Air Power*, which was based on Alexander de Seversky's book of the same name. This film advocated for the strategic importance of air power in winning the war, blending live-action sequences with animation to make a compelling case for modern air warfare tactics.

Disney's personal take on these wartime efforts was marked by a deep sense of patriotism and a desire to contribute to the national cause. Despite his primary identity as an entertainer, Disney recognized the power of animation as a tool for education and propaganda. He believed that his studio could play a crucial role in supporting the war effort by producing content that was not only informative and persuasive but also engaging and accessible to a wide audience.

Although the military films generated sufficient revenue to cover their production costs, Disney faced a financial setback with the release of the feature film *Bambi*. This film, which had been in production since 1937, was released in April 1942. Despite the high hopes for its success, *Bambi* underperformed at the box office, ultimately losing $200,000. The film's financial failure was particularly disappointing given the significant investment of time and resources over its five-year production period. While the military films helped to sustain the studio financially, the loss from *Bambi* highlighted the challenges Disney faced in balancing artistic ambition with commercial viability during the wartime era. Combined with the low earnings from *Pinocchio* and *Fantasia*, the company found itself $4 million in debt with the Bank of America by 1944. In a critical meeting with the bank's executives, chairman Amadeo Giannini expressed his confidence in Disney's future success, advising the executives to give the studio time to market their products.

As the war ended, the Disney Studio faced increasing competition from other animation studios like Warner Bros., and Metro-Goldwyn-Mayer. To diversify their offerings, Roy Disney suggested more combined animation and live-action productions. In 1948, Disney initiated the popular *True-Life Adventures* series of live-action nature films, with *Seal Island* being the first. The film won an Academy Award for Best Short Subject.

In 1949, looking for a change after the war, Walt Disney and his family moved to a new home in the Holmby Hills district of Los Angeles. Inspired by his friends Ward and Betty Kimball, who had their own backyard railroad, Disney embarked

on creating his own miniature live steam railroad. He quickly developed blueprints and set to work on this personal project. He named the railroad the Carolwood Pacific Railroad, after his home's location on Carolwood Drive.

The miniature steam locomotive, which Disney named Lilly Belle in honor of his wife Lillian, was meticulously built by Disney Studios engineer Roger E. Broggie. For three years, the Carolwood Pacific Railroad provided entertainment and joy for Disney and his guests. However, after a series of minor accidents, including a derailment and a guest being scalded by steam, Disney decided to order the locomotive into storage. This personal project not only reflected Disney's love for trains but also showcased his enduring passion for innovation and creativity, even outside the realm of his professional endeavors.

The post-war era also saw Disney exploring new frontiers in entertainment. The studio began to decrease its production of short films, focusing instead on feature-length animations and live-action films. This period of innovation and expansion laid the groundwork for future successes.

As the studio moved into the 1950s, the groundwork laid during the earlier decades allowed for further expansion and diversification. The Disney brothers' ability to adapt to changing circumstances and embrace new opportunities ensured the continued growth and success of the company.

In early 1950, Walt Disney's studio released *Cinderella*, its first animated feature in eight years. The film marked a triumphant return to the full-length animation that had defined Disney's early successes. *Cinderella* was a critical and commercial hit, resonating deeply with both critics and theater audiences. The production cost of $2.2 million was a significant investment, but it paid off handsomely, earning nearly $8 million in its first year. This financial success was a much-needed boost for the studio, reaffirming Disney's ability to create beloved and profitable animated features.

However, Walt Disney's involvement in *Cinderella* was less hands-on compared to his earlier projects. During this period, Disney was increasingly focused on expanding his creative horizons beyond animation. He ventured into the realm of live-action filmmaking with his first entirely live-action feature, *Treasure Island* (1950), which was shot in Britain. This film was followed by *The Story of Robin Hood and His Merrie Men* (1952), also shot in Britain, marking the beginning of a series of live-action adventures that often carried patriotic themes.

Disney's foray into live-action films proved to be successful and broadened the studio's portfolio. This diversification was a strategic move that allowed the company to explore different genres and storytelling techniques, appealing to a wider audience. The live-action features showcased Disney's versatility as a filmmaker and his ability to adapt to new mediums while maintaining the studio's commitment to quality and engaging storytelling.

Despite his growing interest in live-action films, Disney continued to produce full-length animated features. In 1951, the studio released *Alice in Wonderland*, an ambitious adaptation of Lewis Carroll's classic tales. The film was noted for its imaginative animation and whimsical style, capturing the surreal and fantastical elements of the original stories. Following this, *Peter Pan* was released in 1953, bringing J.M. Barrie's timeless tale to life with vibrant animation and memorable characters.

During this period, Disney began to delegate more responsibilities within the animation department. He entrusted most of its operations to his key animators, a talented group known as the Nine Old Men. These animators, including legends like Frank Thomas, Ollie Johnston, and Milt Kahl, were instrumental in shaping the studio's animated features. While Disney was less involved in the day-to-day animation process, he remained a vital presence at story meetings, ensuring that his creative vision was upheld.

As Disney's focus shifted toward new ventures, he also made strategic business moves to strengthen the studio's distribution capabilities. In the early 1950s, Disney established his own film distribution division, Buena Vista Distribution. This decision marked a significant

departure from relying on external distributors like RKO Pictures. By creating Buena Vista, Disney gained greater control over the distribution and marketing of his films, allowing for more strategic release schedules and promotional efforts.

As Walt Disney grew older and his foray into the world expanded, his political views also shifted significantly. Initially a supporter of the Democratic Party, Disney switched his allegiance to the Republican Party during the 1940 presidential election. This marked the beginning of his growing conservatism. By the 1944 presidential election, Disney had become a generous donor to Thomas E. Dewey's campaign for the presidency.

Disney's political involvement deepened in the post-war years. In 1946, he was a founding member of the Motion Picture Alliance for the Preservation of American Ideals. This organization was formed by members of the film industry who believed in the American way of life and were opposed to what they saw as a rising tide of Communism*, Fascism †, and similar ideologies that sought to undermine and change that way of life through subversive means.

In 1947, amid the fervor of the Second Red Scare, Walt Disney testified before the House Un-American Activities Committee (HUAC). The Red Scare was a period of intense fear and suspicion in the United States about communist infiltration and influence. It was

---

* Communism is a political and economic ideology advocating for a classless society in which all property and means of production are collectively owned, eliminating private ownership. Under communism, wealth and resources are distributed according to need, aiming to create economic equality and reduce social disparities. The state plays a central role in planning and controlling the economy, with the goal of abolishing the capitalist system.

† Fascism is a far-right political ideology characterized by dictatorial power, extreme nationalism, and the suppression of opposition. Fascist regimes often emphasize the supremacy of the nation or race, promote aggressive militarism, and maintain strict control over society and the economy. Individual freedoms are typically curtailed, and the state exerts significant influence over many aspects of life, including culture and education.

marked by widespread concern that communists were working to undermine American institutions and values from within. This fear led to heightened political repression and a campaign to identify and remove alleged communists from positions of power and influence. The HUAC committee was established to investigate alleged disloyalty and subversive activities among private citizens, public employees, and organizations suspected of having communist ties.

During his testimony, Disney accused former animators and labor union organizers Herbert Sorrell, David Hilberman, and William Pomerance of being communist agitators. He claimed that these individuals had attempted to undermine his studio by instigating the animators' strike of 1941. This strike, which lasted for several weeks, had a significant impact on Disney's studio, leading to financial losses and internal strife. Disney believed that the strike was not merely a labor dispute but part of a broader, organized effort by communists to gain influence in Hollywood and disrupt American cultural institutions.

Disney's testimony before HUAC was a reflection of his increasing involvement in anti-communist activities and his alignment with the conservative political climate of the time. He asserted that the communist movement was actively working to subvert American values and institutions, using the entertainment industry as a means to spread propaganda and influence public opinion. By naming specific individuals and accusing them of being part of this effort, Disney positioned himself as a staunch opponent of communism.

These political developments occurred alongside significant events in Disney's professional life. While Disney was expanding his political activities and solidifying his conservative views, he continued to innovate and grow his entertainment empire. The period from the late 1940s to the early 1950s was marked by both political engagement and professional achievements, showcasing Disney's multifaceted influence on American culture and politics.

The establishment of Buena Vista was a pivotal move that contributed to the studio's long-term success. It provided Disney with the flexibility to distribute a diverse range of content, including animated features, live-action films, and later, television programs. This control over distribution channels enabled Disney to maximize the profitability of his projects and ensure that his creative works reached the widest possible audience.

During the early to mid-1950s, Disney's diversification into live-action films, the establishment of Buena Vista Distribution, and the conceptualization of Disneyland marked a period of significant growth and transformation for the studio. These ventures showcased Disney's ability to adapt to changing times and explore new opportunities while maintaining the core values of creativity and innovation that defined his brand. Overall, the road to the early 1950s proved to be a transformative period for Walt Disney and his studio.

## We're half way there: A note from Scott Matthews

As we find ourselves at the midpoint of the book, delving deeper into the profound journey of Walt Disney's life, I want to express my sincere gratitude to you. The crafting of this narrative has been a labor of dedication, fueled by a profound reverence for Disney's genius and a commitment to sharing his story with you.

Your engagement and reflections are invaluable not only to me but also to those who seek to comprehend the significance of Disney's legacy. Your reviews not only support my endeavor as a storyteller but also contribute to the collective appreciation of Disney's contributions to entertainment and culture. I take to heart each review, treasuring your perspectives and suggestions for further exploration.

If you have found resonance in the pages thus far or have ideas on how we can navigate the remainder of Disney's journey together, I encourage you to take a moment to share your thoughts. A QR code is provided below for your convenience, which takes you to Amazon where you can leave your review. Whether you are reading digitally or holding a physical copy, a simple scan or click allows you to contribute your reflections.

Thank you for joining in this odyssey. Your feedback not only shapes the narrative but also honors Walt Disney's enduring spirit. Here's to the unfolding chapters and the profound lessons they hold.

# Disneyland: Realizing a Lifelong Dream

Walt Disney's dream of creating a theme park where families could have fun together began to take shape during the early 1950s. Inspired by visits to Griffith Park in Los Angeles with his daughters, Disney envisioned a clean, safe, and imaginative environment that would entertain both children and their parents. His idea was further influenced by a visit to Tivoli Gardens in Copenhagen, Denmark, where he admired the park's cleanliness and layout. These experiences fueled his determination to build a place that combined entertainment with a touch of magic, setting the stage for what would eventually become Disneyland.

In March 1952, Walt Disney received zoning permission to build a theme park in Burbank, near the Disney studios. However, as plans progressed, it quickly became clear that the Burbank site was too small to accommodate the grandeur of Disney's vision. Undeterred by this setback, Disney began searching for a more suitable location that could fulfill his expansive dreams.

After extensive searching, Disney found the ideal site: a 160-acre (6,969,600 square feet or 647,497 square meters) plot of land in Anaheim, thirty-five miles (fifty-six kilometers) south of the studio. This larger location offered the space needed to create a diverse and immersive theme park. To distance this ambitious project from the scrutiny of shareholders and to protect the studio from potential financial risk, Disney formed a new entity, WED Enterprises (now known as Walt Disney Imagineering). By doing so, he could channel his personal funds and creative energy into the project without directly impacting the finances of the Disney studio.

Disney personally funded the initial development and assembled a team of his most talented designers and animators to work on the project. These individuals came to be known as "Imagineers," a term that blended imagination and engineering. The Imagineers were tasked with turning Disney's imaginative concepts into tangible attractions. They brought a wealth of creativity and technical expertise to the project, ensuring that the park would be both innovative and meticulously crafted.

Securing additional funding was crucial for bringing Disneyland to life. Disney approached banks for financial support and also sought investments from other entities. He successfully attracted significant investment from American Broadcasting-Paramount Theatres, part of the American Broadcasting Company (ABC), and Western Printing and Lithographing Company. These partnerships were vital in securing the capital needed to realize his ambitious plans.

By mid-1954, Disney understood the importance of learning from existing amusement parks to create the best possible experience. He sent his Imagineers on a comprehensive research mission to visit every amusement park in the United States. The goal was to analyze their strengths and weaknesses, gather insights on what worked well, and identify common pitfalls to avoid. This extensive research provided invaluable information that shaped the design and operation of Disneyland. The Imagineers' findings highlighted several key elements that were essential for the success of Disneyland. They noted that cleanliness, organization, and attention to detail were critical components of a positive guest experience.

Construction of Disneyland began in July 1954, marking the realization of Walt Disney's grand vision for a place where families could experience joy and wonder together. The design of the park was meticulously planned to create an immersive and magical environment. Disneyland was conceived as a series of themed lands, each with its own distinct atmosphere and attractions, all connected by the central hub of Main Street, U.S., which served as the gateway to the park. This area was a nostalgic replica of the main street in Disney's hometown of Marceline, Missouri. It was designed to evoke the charm and simplicity of small-town America at the turn of the 20th century. Guests entering Disneyland would walk down this beautifully crafted street, lined with quaint shops, eateries, and meticulously detailed buildings, all of which contributed to a sense of stepping back in time.

Beyond Main Street, U.S., visitors could explore the various themed lands, each offering unique attractions and experiences designed to transport them to different worlds. Adventureland was inspired by exotic locales and daring exploits, designed to evoke the spirit of exploration and discovery. It featured lush landscapes, tropical vegetation, and attractions like the Jungle Cruise, where guests could embark on a riverboat adventure through simulated jungles teeming with animatronic animals and thrilling surprises. Frontierland captured the spirit of the American Old West. With its rustic buildings and frontier town ambiance, it offered guests a glimpse into the adventurous and rugged life of pioneers and cowboys. Key attractions included the Mark Twain Riverboat, providing a leisurely cruise along the Rivers of America, and the Frontierland Shootin' Exposition, where visitors could test their sharpshooting skills.

Fantasyland brought beloved fairy tales to life. This area was designed to appeal to the imagination of children and adults alike, featuring iconic attractions such as the Sleeping Beauty Castle, which served as the centerpiece of the park. Other popular rides included Peter Pan's Flight, where guests could soar over London in pirate ships, and the Mad Tea Party, which offered a whimsical spinning teacup experience. Looking to the future, Tomorrowland was a vision of the possibilities that awaited in the world of tomorrow. This land showcased futuristic architecture, space travel, and innovative technology. Attractions like Autopia, where guests could drive their own mini cars, and the Rocket to the Moon, which simulated a trip to outer space, reflected Disney's fascination with progress and innovation.

A unique feature of Disneyland was the narrow-gauge Disneyland Railroad, which encircled the park and connected the various lands. This scenic tour allowed guests to experience the park from a different perspective, offering views of the attractions and landscapes while providing a relaxing break from the hustle and bustle. The train stations in each land were carefully themed to match their respective areas, enhancing the overall immersive experience. To ensure that the magic of Disneyland remained undisturbed by the outside world, a high berm was constructed around the park's perimeter. This berm, essentially a landscaped earthen barrier, helped to block out views and sounds from the surrounding area, creating a sense of separation and immersion. The berm was planted with trees and vegetation, contributing to the park's lush and vibrant appearance while maintaining the illusion of a complete and self-contained world.

On July 17, 1955, Disneyland officially opened its gates. The opening ceremony was a grand event, broadcast live on ABC and reaching an audience of seventy million viewers. The broadcast showcased the park's attractions and highlighted Disney's vision of a magical place for families. Despite some minor problems on opening day, such as technical glitches and overcrowding, Disneyland quickly proved to be a resounding success. An editorial in *The New York Times* praised the park, noting that Disney had "tastefully combined some of the pleasant things of yesterday with fantasy and dreams of tomorrow."

The early success of Disneyland was evident as it attracted over 20,000 visitors per day within a month of opening. By the end of its first year, the park had welcomed 3.6 million guests, far exceeding expectations. This overwhelming popularity confirmed Disney's belief in the potential of a family-friendly theme park and solidified Disneyland's place as a beloved destination for visitors of all ages.

The funding from ABC was dependent upon Disney producing television programs for the network. The studio had previously experienced success with a television special on Christmas Day 1950 about the making of *Alice in Wonderland*. Roy Disney recognized the potential of television as a powerful marketing tool and a source of revenue. In a March 1951 letter to shareholders, he highlighted television's potential to boost box office takings and reach new audiences.

Following the Disneyland funding agreement, ABC began broadcasting *Walt Disney's Disneyland* in 1954. This anthology series featured a mix of animated cartoons, live-action features, and other material from the studio's library. The show quickly became a ratings hit, earning an audience share of over 50%. It was so popular that Newsweek called the series an "American institution" in April 1955. The success of the show also led to Disney's first daily television program, *The Mickey Mouse Club*, a variety show specifically catering to children. This program was accompanied by extensive merchandising, with companies like Western Printing producing coloring books, comics, and other related items.

One particularly successful segment of *Walt Disney's Disneyland* was the five-part miniseries *Davy Crockett*. According to Disney biographer Neal Gabler, the series became an "overnight sensation." The theme song, *The Ballad of Davy Crockett*, became internationally popular, selling ten million records. The immense popularity of the miniseries and its merchandise prompted

Disney to establish his own record production and distribution entity, Disneyland Records.

As Disneyland continued to thrive, Disney's vision for the park expanded. He saw it as a living, breathing entity that would evolve and grow with new attractions and experiences. This philosophy of constant innovation and improvement became a hallmark of Disneyland, ensuring that it remained a dynamic and exciting destination for visitors.

The success of Disneyland also had a profound impact on the local economy. The park created thousands of jobs and spurred the development of hotels, restaurants, and other businesses in the surrounding area. Anaheim transformed from a small agricultural town into a bustling tourist destination, largely thanks to Disneyland's influence. Disneyland's impact extended beyond its immediate surroundings. It set a new standard for theme parks and inspired similar projects around the world.

As the 1950s progressed, Disney continued to expand his entertainment empire. He explored new opportunities in television, film, and other media, always pushing the boundaries of what was possible. The success of Disneyland provided the financial stability and creative freedom to pursue these ventures, allowing Disney to bring his unique brand of magic to an ever-growing audience.

Walt Disney's journey through the 1950s and 1960s was marked by remarkable technological advances and significant corporate growth, transforming his company into a global entertainment powerhouse. Alongside the construction and subsequent success of Disneyland, Disney ventured into numerous other projects that showcased his visionary approach and commitment to innovation.

In the mid-1950s, Walt Disney's attention was indeed divided between his burgeoning theme park, Disneyland, and various groundbreaking projects that demonstrated his commitment to innovation and education. One particularly notable project during this time was the *Man in Space* episode of the Disneyland television series, which aired in 1955. This episode was a remarkable collaboration with NASA rocket designer Wernher von Braun and was part of Disney's broader effort to educate the public about space exploration.

The idea for *Man in Space* stemmed from Disney's fascination with science and his desire to use the power of television to inspire and inform the public about the possibilities of space travel. At a time when space exploration was still in its infancy and the space race between the United States and the Soviet Union was heating up, Disney saw an opportunity to leverage his platform to contribute to the national conversation about space.

To bring this ambitious project to life, Disney enlisted the expertise of Wernher von Braun, a key figure in rocket technology and space science. Von Braun had been instrumental in the development of rocket technology during World War II and had subsequently become a leading advocate for space exploration in the United States. His involvement lent the project a significant degree of scientific credibility.

*Man in Space* was designed to be both educational and entertaining, adhering to Disney's philosophy of "edutainment." The episode aimed to demystify the complexities of rocket science and space travel, making them accessible to a broad audience. It combined live-action segments, animation, and actual footage of rocket launches to create a comprehensive and engaging narrative.

The episode began with Walt Disney himself introducing the topic and explaining the significance of space exploration. This personal touch helped to establish a connection with the audience and set the stage for the educational journey that followed. The narrative then transitioned to animated segments that illustrated the basic principles of rocketry, such as the forces of thrust and gravity.

One of the most innovative aspects of *Man in Space* was its use of animation to explain complex scientific concepts. Disney's animators, known for their creativity and technical prowess, created detailed and visually engaging sequences that depicted the mechanics of rocket propulsion and the challenges of space travel. These animations were complemented by live-action segments featuring von Braun, who provided expert commentary and insights.

Von Braun's presence was a key element of the episode's success. His ability to explain technical concepts in a clear and compelling manner helped to bridge the gap between scientific theory and practical application. He discussed the history of rocketry, the current state of space technology, and the future possibilities of space exploration, all while emphasizing the potential benefits for humanity.

The climax of the episode was a speculative look at what a manned mission to space might look like. Using a combination of animation and live-action, the episode depicted a fictional but scientifically grounded scenario in which astronauts were launched into space, orbited the Earth, and safely returned. This visionary portrayal captured the imagination of viewers and provided a tantalizing glimpse of what the future might hold.

*Man in Space* was a resounding success, both in terms of ratings and impact. It drew a large audience, captivated by the blend of education and entertainment that Disney had masterfully orchestrated.

Following the success of *Man in Space*, Disney produced two more space-themed episodes: *Man and the Moon* and *Mars and Beyond*. These episodes continued the exploration of space science and further solidified Disney's role as a pioneer in educational television. Each episode built upon the foundation laid by *Man in Space*, using a similar blend of animation, live-action, and expert commentary to engage and inform viewers.

During this period, Disney was also deeply involved in the production of several full-length animated features. In 1955, the Disney studio released *Lady and the Tramp*, marking a significant milestone in animation history. *Lady and the Tramp* was the first  animated film to be produced in CinemaScope, a widescreen process that allowed for a much broader aspect ratio. This technological innovation enabled animators to create more expansive and immersive scenes, enhancing the storytelling experience. The use of CinemaScope presented a challenge for the animators, who had to adapt to the wider frame, ensuring that the compositions remained visually engaging and balanced. The film's story of an upper-class Cocker Spaniel named Lady who falls in love with a street-smart mutt named Tramp was brought to life with greater depth and detail, thanks to this new technology.

The success of *Lady and the Tramp* was significant not only for its technological achievements but also for its storytelling and emotional resonance. The film's charming narrative, memorable characters, and beautiful animation captivated audiences and critics alike. Its innovative use of CinemaScope demonstrated Disney's forward-thinking approach and his commitment to leveraging the latest technologies to enhance the cinematic experience. This film proved that animated features could be more than just children's entertainment; they could also appeal to a broad audience through sophisticated storytelling and technical excellence.

The late 1950s continued to be a period of technological advancement for Disney with the release of *Sleeping Beauty* in 1959. This film represented another leap forward in animation technology, as it was the first animated feature to be produced in Technirama 70 mm film. Technirama was a widescreen process that provided unprecedented visual clarity and detail, allowing for richly detailed backgrounds and more dynamic compositions. This format offered a higher resolution and greater depth of field, making the visuals of *Sleeping Beauty* more striking and immersive.

*Sleeping Beauty* was notable for its distinct artistic style, heavily influenced by the medieval art and tapestries of the period in which the story is set. The film's art director, Eyvind Earle, played a crucial role in developing this unique look. Earle's backgrounds were highly stylized, with intricate details and a palette of rich, vibrant colors that added to the film's fairy-tale quality. The characters were designed to complement these backgrounds, creating a cohesive and visually stunning aesthetic.

Despite its artistic achievements, *Sleeping Beauty* was initially a financial disappointment. The film's production had been costly and lengthy, taking nearly a decade to complete. Upon its release, it did not perform as well at the box office as expected, which was a setback for the studio. However, over time, *Sleeping Beauty* gained recognition and appreciation for its artistic merit and technical innovation. It has since become a classic, celebrated for its unique visual style and its contributions to the art of animation.

The advancements in *Sleeping Beauty* set new standards for the industry. The use of Technirama 70 mm film pushed the boundaries of what was possible in animation, encouraging other studios to explore similar technologies. The film's elaborate animation and richly detailed backgrounds demonstrated the potential of animation to create immersive and visually compelling worlds.

Disney's involvement in these films during the mid to late 1950s underscored his unwavering commitment to pushing the boundaries of animation. By embracing new technologies like CinemaScope and Technirama, he was able to elevate the art form, creating more immersive and visually stunning films. These advancements were not merely technical achievements; they also enhanced the storytelling, allowing for more dynamic and engaging narratives.

In addition to his film projects, Walt Disney served as a consultant for the 1959 American National Exhibition in Moscow, an event designed to showcase American culture, technology, and achievements to the Soviet Union. One of the standout contributions from Disney Studios to the exhibition was the film *America the Beautiful*, presented in a groundbreaking 360-degree Circarama theater.

The Circarama Theater was an innovative format developed by Disney's team, featuring a circular screen that surrounded the audience. This unique design allowed viewers to be completely immersed in the imagery, providing a panoramic view  that was unlike anything they had experienced before. The theater was equipped with multiple synchronized projectors, each displaying a segment of the film on different sections of the circular screen. The seamless integration of these segments created a continuous, enveloping visual experience.

The immersive nature of *America the Beautiful* began as soon as visitors entered the Circarama Theater. Unlike traditional theaters, where the screen is confined to one wall, the Circarama's circular screen encircled the audience, filling their entire field of vision. This setup meant that viewers were not just watching a film; they were placed at the center of the action, with scenes unfolding all around them.

The film itself was a visual journey across the diverse landscapes of the United States, showcasing its natural beauty, bustling cities, and iconic landmarks. The 360-degree format allowed for sweeping vistas and dynamic movement, capturing everything from the grandeur of the Grand Canyon to the skyline of New York City. The scenes were meticulously crafted to utilize the full potential of the circular screen, with carefully choreographed shots that guided the audience's gaze around the theater.

To enhance the immersive experience, the film incorporated carefully designed audio to complement the visuals. The surround sound system was synchronized with the imagery, providing directional audio cues that further immersed viewers in the environment. For example, the roar of Niagara Falls would seem to come from the appropriate direction as it appeared on screen, and the hustle and bustle of city streets surrounded the audience, making them feel as if they were right in the midst of the action.

The combination of panoramic visuals and directional audio created a multi-sensory experience that captivated the audience. *America the Beautiful* was not just a film; it was an experiential journey that transported viewers to different parts of the United States. This immersive quality made the attraction one of the most popular exhibits at the American National Exhibition, drawing large crowds and widespread acclaim.

Disney's use of the Circarama Theater highlighted his ability to harness technology to create engaging and memorable experiences. The 360-degree format was a precursor to modern immersive media and virtual reality, showcasing Disney's forward-thinking approach and his commitment to pushing the boundaries of storytelling and entertainment.

The success of *America the Beautiful* at the exhibition underscored Disney's talent for combining innovative technology with compelling content. It also reinforced his reputation as a master storyteller who could captivate audiences through new and exciting formats.

The following year, Disney's expertise was sought for the 1960 Winter Olympics in Squaw Valley, California. As the chairman of the Pageantry Committee, he designed the opening, closing, and medal ceremonies. Disney's involvement ensured that these events were not only well-organized but also infused with a sense of spectacle and magic that became a hallmark of his brand.

In 1960, Disney expanded his business interests by becoming one of twelve investors in the Celebrity Sports Center in Glendale, Colorado. This family-oriented entertainment complex featured bowling alleys, swimming pools, and an ice rink. By 1962, Disney and his brother Roy had bought out the other investors, making the Disney company the sole owner. The acquisition of the Celebrity Sports Center was part of Disney's broader strategy to diversify his entertainment offerings and create new revenue streams.

Throughout these years, Disney continued to innovate in the realm of animation. In 1961, the studio released *One Hundred and One Dalmatians*, the first animated feature to use Xerox cels*. This technique allowed animators to transfer their drawings directly onto the cels, eliminating the need for hand-inking and significantly reducing production costs. The success of *One Hundred and One*

---

* Xerox cels are a significant innovation in the history of animation, introduced by Disney Studios in the early 1960s to streamline the animation process and reduce production costs. The introduction of Xerox cels revolutionized this workflow in animation. Xerox cels utilized a Xerox photocopying process to transfer animators' drawings directly onto the celluloid sheets, eliminating the need for hand-inking.

*Dalmatians* demonstrated the effectiveness of this new process and its potential to streamline animation production by reducing both time and money required for production.

The early 1960s also saw the release of *The Sword in the Stone* in 1963. While not as groundbreaking as some of Disney's earlier works, it continued the studio's tradition of high-quality animation and storytelling. During this time, Disney was already setting his sights on more ambitious projects.

In 1964, Walt Disney achieved one of his most significant cinematic successes with the release of *Mary Poppins*. This film, based on the beloved book series by P. L. Travers had been a project Disney pursued with unwavering determination since the 1940s. Travers' stories about the magical nanny, Mary Poppins, had captivated Disney, and he was convinced that her tales would make for a compelling and enchanting film. However, securing the rights from Travers proved to be a prolonged and challenging endeavor, spanning nearly two decades.

Travers was notoriously protective of her work and had numerous reservations about adapting her books into a film. She feared that her carefully crafted characters and the British essence of her stories would be lost in translation. Disney's persistence, charm, and vision eventually won her over, although she retained significant control over the script and creative decisions.

*Mary Poppins* combined live-action and animation in a way that had never been done before, setting a new benchmark for cinematic innovation. The film featured groundbreaking sequences where live actors interact seamlessly with animated characters and environments. One of the most iconic scenes involved Mary Poppins (Julie Andrews) and Bert (Dick Van Dyke) dancing with animated penguins, a sequence that required meticulous choreography and pioneering special effects. This blend of live-action and animation created a magical and memorable experience for audiences, transporting them to a whimsical world where anything was possible.

The film's narrative was both heartwarming and fantastical, centering around the Banks family in Edwardian London. Mary Poppins, the mysterious and magical nanny, arrives to care for the Banks children, bringing with her a sense of wonder and adventure that transforms their lives. The film's story was infused with lessons about family, imagination, and the importance of joy, resonating deeply with viewers of all ages.

*Mary Poppins* was more than just a technical marvel; it was a triumph of storytelling, music, and performance. Julie Andrews' portrayal of Mary Poppins was widely acclaimed, earning her an Academy Award for Best Actress. Her performance combined warmth, authority, and a touch of magic, perfectly embodying the character from Travers' books. Dick Van Dyke's role as Bert, the cheerful chimney sweep, also received praise, despite some criticism of his British accent. Van Dyke's infectious energy and charm brought a delightful balance to the film.

The music of *Mary Poppins*, composed by Richard M. Sherman and Robert B. Sherman, became one of the film's standout elements. The soundtrack featured memorable songs like *A Spoonful of Sugar*, *Chim Chim Cher-ee*, *Supercalifragilisticexpialidocious*, and *Feed the Birds*. These songs not only advanced the narrative but also became timeless classics, contributing significantly to the film's enduring popularity. The Sherman Brothers' work earned them two Academy Awards: one for Best Original Score and one for Best Original Song (*Chim Chim Cher-ee*).

Despite its overwhelming success, *Mary Poppins* was not without controversy. P. L. Travers was famously dissatisfied with several aspects of the film. She disapproved of the animation sequences, felt the character of Mary Poppins was softened, and was unhappy with the musical elements. Travers' dissatisfaction was so profound that she refused to allow any further adaptations of her works by Disney. Nevertheless, the film's reception and impact overshadowed her criticisms.

*Mary Poppins* became the most successful Disney film of the 1960s, earning widespread critical acclaim and numerous awards. It was nominated for thirteen Academy Awards and won five, including Best Actress for Julie Andrews, Best Film Editing, Best Original Music Score, Best Visual Effects, and Best Original Song. The film's success was a testament to Disney's ability to adapt beloved literature into a universally appealing cinematic experience.

The success of *Mary Poppins* cemented Disney's reputation as a master storyteller and a pioneer in the entertainment industry. It demonstrated his unique talent for blending different media and technologies to create a cohesive and captivating narrative. The film's innovative use of special effects, combined with its strong performances and memorable music, set a new standard for family entertainment.

That same year, Disney became involved in plans to expand the California Institute of the Arts, commonly known as CalArts. He envisioned the institute as a place where artists from various disciplines could come together to learn and collaborate. Disney had an architect draw up blueprints for a new building, reflecting his commitment to fostering creativity and innovation in future generations of artists.

Throughout the 1950s and 1960s, Disney's work extended far beyond the studio and theme park. He continued to push the boundaries of technology and creativity, ensuring that his company remained at the forefront of the entertainment industry. His involvement in diverse projects, from educational television programs to the organization of major public events, showcased his versatility and ability to adapt to new challenges.

Despite the increasing demands of these various projects, Disney never lost sight of his primary goal: to entertain and inspire audiences. His relentless pursuit of excellence and innovation drove the technological advances and corporate growth that characterized this period. Each new venture built upon the successes of the past, creating a legacy of innovation that would influence the industry for decades to come.

Disney's influence extended significantly to television, where his shows continued to captivate audiences and shape the medium. One of the most groundbreaking ventures was *Walt Disney's Disneyland*, an anthology series that debuted in 1954. This series was designed to serve multiple purposes: it promoted the new Disneyland theme park, showcased Disney's vast library of content, and demonstrated the potential of television as a powerful entertainment medium. The show included a mix of animated cartoons, live-action features, and other material from the studio's extensive library, creating a diverse and engaging viewing experience.

*Walt Disney's Disneyland* quickly became a ratings sensation, earning an audience share of over 50%. Its success underscored Disney's ability to connect with viewers of all ages and made the series an integral part of American culture. The show's popularity helped solidify Disney's dominance in the television market and proved that television could be a lucrative platform for the studio's content.

The success of *Walt Disney's Disneyland* led to the creation of *The Mickey Mouse Club*, a variety show specifically catering to children. Premiering in 1955, *The Mickey Mouse Club* featured a cast of talented young performers known as the  Mouseketeers, along with animated segments, musical numbers, and serialized adventures. The show's catchy theme song, *M-I-C-K-E-Y M-O-U-S-E*, became iconic, and the program quickly garnered a massive following. *The Mickey Mouse Club* not only entertained children but also reinforced Disney's brand, creating a loyal audience that would continue to engage with Disney products for years to come.

One of the most notable segments of *Walt Disney's Disneyland* was the five-part miniseries *Davy Crockett*. This series chronicled the adventures of the legendary frontiersman, played by actor Fess Parker. *Davy Crockett* became an overnight sensation, capturing the imagination of viewers with its tales of bravery and exploration. The series was so popular that it sparked a nationwide craze for Davy Crockett-themed merchandise, including coonskin caps, toy rifles, and action figures.

The theme song of the series, *The Ballad of Davy Crockett*, became internationally popular, with its catchy lyrics and memorable melody. The song's refrain, "Born on a mountaintop in Tennessee, greenest state in the land of the free," resonated with audiences and contributed to the character's legendary status. The ballad sold ten million records, demonstrating the incredible reach and influence of the series.

The immense popularity of *Davy Crockett* and its associated merchandise prompted Disney to form his own record production and distribution entity, Disneyland Records, in 1956. This strategic move allowed Disney to capitalize on the success of his television shows and expand his company's reach into the music industry. Disneyland Records produced and distributed a wide range of recordings, including soundtracks from Disney films, television shows, and original music inspired by Disney characters and stories.

The creation of Disneyland Records further solidified Disney's dominance in the entertainment industry, enabling the company to control the production and distribution of its music content. This vertical integration ensured that Disney could maximize profits from its popular songs and soundtracks while maintaining high quality and consistency across its products.

As Disney's corporate empire grew, so did his influence on American culture. He was able to leverage his success in film, television, and theme parks to create a cohesive and multifaceted entertainment empire. Each new venture reinforced the others, creating a synergistic effect that amplified the impact of his work.

The late 1950s and early 1960s were a period of remarkable technological advances and corporate growth for Disney. His ability to integrate new technologies into his projects, whether in film, television, or theme parks, set new standards for the industry. The success of these ventures demonstrated Disney's unique talent for combining creativity with business acumen, ensuring that his company remained at the forefront of the entertainment world.

Disney's impact on the entertainment industry was profound and far-reaching. His willingness to embrace new technologies and explore new avenues of storytelling transformed the way audiences experienced film, television, and theme parks.

Walt Disney's years of recognition, particularly during the 1960s, were marked by a series of ambitious projects, innovative advancements, and significant personal achievements. This period encapsulated Disney's relentless pursuit of excellence and his commitment to creating experiences that would delight audiences around the world.

In the early 1960s, Disney's creative energies were channeled into several high-profile projects, including his contributions to the 1964 New York World's Fair. This event provided Disney with a unique platform to showcase his technological innovations and storytelling prowess. For the fair, he developed four major exhibits, each backed by corporate sponsors who recognized Disney's unparalleled ability to captivate and educate audiences.

One of the standout exhibits that Walt Disney developed for the 1964 New York World's Fair was "It's a Small World," sponsored by

PepsiCo as a tribute to **UNICEF**. This attraction featured a whimsical boat ride through various scenes depicting children from around the globe, brought to life through audio-animatronic dolls. Designed by Disney's team of talented Imagineers, including the artist Mary Blair, the ride was a vibrant, colorful celebration of cultural diversity and global unity. Each scene featured dolls dressed in traditional costumes, singing the now-iconic theme song, *It's a Small World (After All)*, written by the Sherman Brothers. The song's repetitive, cheerful melody and simple, heartfelt message of peace and harmony became an enduring anthem of global unity and peace. The attraction's simplicity and charm, combined with its innovative use of audio-animatronics, made it an instant hit with fairgoers. Its popularity was so immense that it ensured "It's a Small World" would become a permanent fixture at Disneyland after the fair, where it continued to enchant visitors with its timeless message of unity.

Another significant exhibit at the fair was "Great Moments with Mr. Lincoln" sponsored by the State of Illinois. This attraction showcased an animatronic Abraham Lincoln delivering excerpts from his most famous speeches, such as the Gettysburg Address. This exhibit was particularly noteworthy for its lifelike representation of Lincoln, made possible by Disney's pioneering use of audio-animatronics. The animatronic Lincoln was a marvel of engineering and craftsmanship, capable of realistic movements and facial expressions. "Great Moments with Mr. Lincoln" captivated audiences with its impressive lifelike portrayal, and like "It's a Small World," it later found a permanent home at Disneyland.

"Carousel of Progress," sponsored by General Electric, was another highlight of Disney's contributions to the World's Fair. This rotating theater presentation chronicled the evolution of technology and its impact on the American family across several decades. The show was divided into acts, each depicting a different era in American history, showcasing the technological advancements that defined each period. The carousel theater allowed the audience to remain seated while the stages rotated around them, revealing each new scene in turn. The presentation emphasized the importance of electricity and innovation, resonating with audiences through its optimistic vision of the future. The exhibit's catchy theme song, *There's a Great Big Beautiful Tomorrow*, also written by the Sherman Brothers, encapsulated Disney's forward-looking philosophy.

Another groundbreaking attraction was Ford's "Magic Skyway," developed by Disney for the World's Fair. This ride took guests on a journey through time, showcasing the progress of mankind from prehistoric times to the future. Visitors traveled in actual Ford automobiles along a track that moved them through a series of elaborate dioramas and animated scenes. The journey began with scenes of dinosaurs and early humans, progressed through ancient civilizations like Rome and the Renaissance, and concluded with a futuristic vision of tomorrow. The ride's innovative use of real cars on a continuous track system was a precursor to similar ride systems that would later be used in Disney theme parks.

These exhibits not only highlighted Disney's innovative spirit but also laid the groundwork for future attractions at Disneyland. Many of the concepts and technologies developed for the World's Fair were later integrated into the theme park, ensuring their continued impact on visitors.

During this period, Disney also explored ambitious plans beyond theme parks. He developed proposals for a ski resort in Mineral King, a glacial valley in California's Sierra Nevada. Disney hired experts like the renowned Olympic ski coach and ski-area designer Willy Schaeffler to bring this vision to life. However, despite significant planning and development, the project faced numerous environmental and regulatory challenges, ultimately preventing its realization.

As Disneyland's success grew, Disney continued to seek new venues for his creative ventures. In 1963, he presented a project to create a theme park in downtown St. Louis, Missouri. Initially, he reached an agreement with the Civic Center Redevelopment Corporation, which controlled the land. However, the deal later collapsed over funding disputes, illustrating the financial and logistical hurdles that often accompanied Disney's grand ambitions.

Undeterred, Disney turned his attention to an even more ambitious project: the development of Disney World in Florida. Announced in late 1965, Disney World was envisioned as a vast entertainment complex southwest of Orlando. The centerpiece of this new venture was the "Magic Kingdom," a larger and more elaborate version of Disneyland. The project also included plans for golf courses, resort hotels, and other recreational facilities.

At the heart of Disney World was the "Experimental Prototype Community of Tomorrow" (EPCOT). Disney described EPCOT as "an experimental prototype community of tomorrow that will take its cue from the new ideas and new  technologies that are now emerging from the creative centers of American industry." He envisioned it as a continuously evolving community that would showcase innovative materials and systems, serving as a testament to American ingenuity and imagination.

Throughout 1966, Disney actively cultivated business partnerships to sponsor EPCOT. He engaged with various industries to secure the necessary support and funding for this ambitious project. Disney's vision for EPCOT reflected his deep belief in the power of creativity and technology to improve society and inspire progress.

In addition to his large-scale projects, Disney remained deeply involved in film production. In 1966, he received a story credit for the film *Lt. Robin Crusoe, U.S.N.* under the pseudonym Retlaw Yensid, a playful backward spelling of his name. This period also saw Disney heavily involved in the development of several significant films, including the animated feature *The Jungle Book*, the live-action musical *The Happiest Millionaire*, and the animated short *Winnie the Pooh and the Blustery Day*. His hands-on approach to storytelling and production ensured that each film met the high standards of quality and entertainment that audiences had come to expect from Disney.

On the personal front, Walt Disney's life during these years was a blend of professional achievements and personal challenges. Despite the demands of his career, Disney remained devoted to his family. He and his wife, Lillian, shared a close bond and took pride in their daughters, Diane and Sharon. The couple's private life was kept largely out of the public eye, a deliberate choice to ensure their family's privacy and security.

As the 1960s progressed, Walt Disney continued to pursue his relentless quest for innovation and excellence in entertainment. However, these years were also marked by significant personal challenges, particularly related to his health. Disney, a heavy smoker since World War I, had long been known for his unfiltered cigarettes and occasional pipe smoking. By the mid-1960s, these habits caught up with him.

In early November 1966, Walt Disney was diagnosed with lung cancer. The news was devastating, but Disney, ever the optimist, sought treatment immediately. He underwent cobalt therapy, a form of radiation treatment that was cutting-edge at the time. Despite the seriousness of his condition, Disney continued to work on his numerous projects, displaying the same determination and passion that had driven him throughout his career.

On November 30, 1966, Disney felt unwell and was taken by ambulance from his home to St. Joseph Hospital in Burbank, California. Despite the best efforts of his medical team, his condition deteriorated rapidly. On December 15, 1966, at the age of sixty-five, Walt Disney passed away due to circulatory collapse caused by cancer. His death marked the end of an era, leaving behind a legacy that would continue to influence the world of entertainment for generations to come. Two days after his death, Disney's remains were cremated, and his ashes were interred at the Forest Lawn Memorial Park in Glendale, California.

Contrary to popular belief, Disney was not cryogenically frozen, The conspiracy theory that Walt Disney's body was frozen and buried beneath Disneyland has intrigued many for decades. This rumor likely originated around the time of his death in 1966, coinciding with the early public interest in cryonics. The first human cryonic freezing occurred just a month after Disney's death, which fueled speculation. The fact that Disney's funeral was private and his cremation was not widely publicized added to the mystery.

The rumor spread through urban legends, word-of-mouth, and sensationalist media, further amplified by unauthorized biographies and tabloid articles in the 1960s and 1970s. These sources often speculated about Disney's fascination with futuristic technology and his secretive personality, thus embedding the idea in popular culture.

Despite repeated official statements from Disney's family and the Walt Disney Company, as well as documented evidence showing that Disney was cremated and his ashes interred at Forest Lawn Memorial Park in Glendale, California, the myth persists. The cryonics community also confirms that Disney had no known interest in cryonics.

In the wake of Disney's passing, his final projects were brought to completion by the dedicated team he had built over the years. One of the most notable releases was *The Jungle Book* in 1967. This animated feature, based on Rudyard Kipling's classic stories, was the last film that Walt Disney personally oversaw. The movie was a critical and commercial success, beloved for its vibrant characters, catchy songs, and engaging story. It became a tribute to Disney's enduring influence on animation and storytelling.

*The Happiest Millionaire*, a live-action musical, was also released in 1967, further showcasing Disney's diverse interests in different forms of entertainment. With these two films, the total number of feature films Disney had been involved in reached an impressive eighty-one. Despite his absence, Disney's vision and standards continued to guide the studio's output.

In 1968, the release of *Winnie the Pooh and the Blustery Day* brought further recognition to Disney's legacy. This animated short won an Academy Award in the Short Subject (Cartoon) category, awarded posthumously to Walt Disney. The film's success underscored the timeless appeal of Disney's beloved characters and the enduring quality of the studio's work.

After Walt's death in 1966, his brother Roy O. Disney assumed full control of The Walt Disney Company till his death in 1971, when he was seventy-eight years old. Roy became the de facto leader and was responsible for overseeing the company's operations and ensuring Walt's vision continued. Roy's dedication ensured the company's stability and growth during challenging times, solidifying his legacy as a key architect of the Disney empire. His strategic decisions and unwavering support were fundamental to the company's enduring success, making him an indispensable figure in the history of The Walt Disney Company.

Overall, Roy played a pivotal role in the success and growth of The Walt Disney Company both in Walt's life and after his death, often operating behind the scenes while his brother Walt took the spotlight. As the co-founder, Roy was instrumental in managing the business and financial aspects of the company, allowing Walt to focus on the creative side. His financial acumen and careful management were crucial in securing funding for their ambitious projects, including the construction of Disneyland.

However, after Disney's death, his studio faced challenges. While the company continued to produce live-action films prolifically, the quality of their animated features began to decline. It wasn't until the late 1980s that this trend was reversed, heralding what *The New York Times* described as the "Disney Renaissance." This period began with the release of *The Little Mermaid* in 1989, which revitalized the studio's animation division and led to a series of critically acclaimed and commercially successful films, including *Beauty and the Beast*, *Aladdin*, and *The Lion King*.

By 2014, Disney theme parks around the world were hosting approximately 134 million visitors annually, a clear indication of the lasting appeal of Disney's creations. The parks continued to evolve, incorporating new technologies and attractions that reflected Disney's original vision of a dynamic, ever-changing entertainment experience.

Throughout his life, Walt Disney was driven by a relentless pursuit of creativity and excellence. His final years were no exception, as he continued to push boundaries and explore new ideas, even in the face of personal health challenges. Disney's dedication to his work and his unwavering belief in the power of imagination left an indelible mark on the world, ensuring that his legacy would endure long after his passing.

The period leading up to Disney's death was marked by several significant projects that demonstrated his continued innovation and ambition. His work on the 1964 New York World's Fair exhibits, such as "It's a Small World," "Great Moments with Mr. Lincoln," "Carousel of Progress," and Ford's "Magic Skyway," showcased his ability to combine technology and storytelling in groundbreaking ways. These exhibits not only delighted fairgoers but also set the stage for future attractions at Disneyland and other Disney parks.

Disney's vision extended beyond theme parks and film. He developed ambitious plans for a ski resort in Mineral King, a glacial valley in California's Sierra Nevada. Although the project faced numerous obstacles and was ultimately never realized, it demonstrated Disney's continued commitment to creating innovative and diverse entertainment experiences.

In addition to his professional endeavors, Disney's personal life during his final years was filled with both joy and hardship. Despite his declining health, he remained deeply connected to his family. The Disney family's privacy was carefully maintained, with Walt ensuring that his loved ones were shielded from the public eye as much as possible.

After Walt Disney's death, Lillian Disney also played a significant role in preserving and promoting his legacy. As Walt's widow, she was deeply involved in various projects and initiatives that aimed to honor his memory and continue his vision for the Walt Disney Company. Lillian's dedication to her late husband's dreams was evident in her support for the development of Walt Disney World in Florida, which opened in 1971. This ambitious project had been one of Walt's final major undertakings, and Lillian's involvement ensured that it reflected his innovative spirit and commitment to family entertainment.

Lillian also contributed to the preservation of Walt's personal and professional history. She was instrumental in the establishment of the Walt Disney Family Museum in San Francisco, which opened in 2009. Although Lillian Disney did not live to see its completion, having passed away in 1997 at the age of ninety-eight, her initial support and contributions were crucial in bringing the museum to fruition. The museum was designed by Disney's daughter Diane and her son, Walter E. D. Miller, and it houses thousands of artifacts from Disney's life and career. This provides visitors with an in-depth look at his journey and accomplishments. The museum includes numerous awards that Disney received, offering a testament to his impact on the entertainment industry and popular culture.

The museum serves as a comprehensive tribute to Walt's life, showcasing his achievements and the profound impact he had on the entertainment industry. Lillian's efforts helped create a space where future generations could learn about  and be inspired by Walt Disney's enduring legacy.

Beyond her direct involvement in projects, Lillian's philanthropic activities also reflected her commitment to honoring Walt's memory. She supported numerous charitable causes, particularly those related to the arts and education, areas that were close to Walt's heart. She made significant donations to institutions such as the California Institute of the Arts and the Los Angeles Music Center. Through her donations and active participation in various organizations, Lillian ensured that Walt's values and passions continued to make a positive impact on society. Her unwavering dedication to upholding and advancing her husband's vision cemented Lillian Disney's role as a key guardian of the Disney legacy.

She continued to live a life marked by grace and quiet philanthropy. She largely stayed out of the public eye, focusing on her family and personal interests. In her later years, Lillian enjoyed spending time with her daughters, Diane and Sharon, and her grandchildren, maintaining the close-knit family values that she and Walt had cherished. Despite the enormous legacy left by her husband, Lillian remained humble and dedicated to preserving his memory through her philanthropic efforts.

Walt Disney's death was a profound loss to the world of entertainment. However, his spirit and vision lived on through the efforts of his wife, his brother Roy, and the dedicated team at Disney Studios. His descendants have also continued to play a role in maintaining this legacy.

Abigail Disney and Roy E. Disney, both descendants of the Disney family, have made significant contributions to The Walt Disney Company and beyond, each in their unique ways. Abigail Disney, the granddaughter of Roy O. Disney, is a documentary filmmaker, philanthropist, and vocal activist. She is known for her advocacy for social justice, economic equality, and corporate responsibility. Abigail has been particularly outspoken about the pay disparity within The Walt Disney Company, advocating for better wages and working conditions for employees. She uses her platform to address broader issues of economic inequality and social justice, extending her influence beyond her family's legacy.

Roy E. Disney, the nephew of Walt Disney and son of Roy O. Disney, played a crucial role in the company's history. As a senior executive and board member, he was instrumental in several significant corporate decisions. Most notably, Roy E. Disney led the "Save Disney" campaign in the early 2000s, which was pivotal in the resignation of then-CEO Michael Eisner. His efforts were driven by a desire to realign the company with its founding principles and creative vision. Roy was also a driving force behind the revitalization of Disney's animation studios, contributing to the renaissance period that produced classics like *The Little Mermaid* and *The Lion King*. His dedication to preserving the Disney legacy and his strategic influence left an indelible mark on the company.

In the decades since Disney's death, the company he founded has continued to grow and evolve, maintaining the high standards of creativity and innovation that he established. Disney's influence can be seen in every aspect of the entertainment industry, from film and television to theme parks and beyond. His commitment to storytelling, technology, and imagination has left a lasting mark on the world, ensuring that his legacy will continue to inspire future generations.

Walt Disney's final projects and days were a reflection of his unwavering dedication to his work and his vision for the future. Despite facing significant health challenges, he continued to push the boundaries of what was possible, creating experiences that would delight and inspire audiences for years to come. His legacy lives on through the countless people who continue to be inspired by his creativity, innovation, and belief in the power of imagination.

# The Enduring Legacy of Walt Disney

Walt Disney's legacy is an intricate fabric woven from groundbreaking creativity, technological innovation, and a personal life that has intrigued and inspired millions. Understanding Disney's enduring impact involves understanding his public persona versus his private self, and the mixed views on his contributions to culture and entertainment.

Despite his professional success, Walt Disney's personal life was complex and often at odds with his public persona. To the public, Disney was the epitome of creativity, charm, and innovation – a charismatic figure who brought joy to millions. However, those who knew him personally or worked closely with him saw a different side.

Playwright Robert E. Sherwood described Disney as "almost painfully shy... diffident" and self-deprecating. This was a stark contrast to the confident and outgoing image he projected in public. According to his biographer Richard Schickel, Disney hid his shy and insecure personality behind his public identity. This public identity was meticulously crafted and maintained, serving as a protective shield that allowed Disney to navigate the pressures of fame and business.

Disney's colleague and animator Ward Kimball noted that Disney "played the role of a bashful tycoon who was embarrassed in public" and was fully aware of doing so. This self-awareness highlights Disney's understanding of the need to cultivate a certain image to sustain his brand and influence. He once confided to a friend, "I'm not Walt Disney. I do a lot of things Walt Disney would not do. Walt Disney does not smoke. I smoke. Walt Disney does not drink. I drink." This admission underscores the dichotomy between the man and the persona – Walt Disney, the public figure, was a carefully curated character distinct from the private individual.

Critic Otis Ferguson, writing for *The New Republic*, described the private Disney as "common and everyday, not inaccessible, not in a foreign language, not suppressed or sponsored or anything. Just Disney." This characterization paints a picture of a man who, away from the limelight, was down-to-earth and relatable, far removed from the larger-than-life image he portrayed.

Disney's approach to managing his staff also reflected his complex personality. Many who worked with him commented that he gave his staff little direct encouragement due to his exceptionally high expectations. Animator Frank Thomas recalled that when Disney said "That'll work," it was considered high praise. This brief and understated acknowledgment was often the most overt form of approval his employees received. Instead of lavish praise, Disney preferred to show his appreciation through actions rather than words.

Instead of direct verbal approval, Disney often rewarded high-performing staff with financial bonuses or by recommending them to others. This indirect method of recognition was his way of expressing gratitude and encouragement. Disney believed that financial rewards and professional opportunities were more meaningful and motivating than words alone. This approach, while effective for some, also created an environment where staff had to interpret his often minimal feedback and derive their motivation from his rare but impactful gestures of approval.

Disney's exceptionally high standards and indirect management style could be both inspiring and challenging. Employees were driven to meet his expectations, knowing that even a small nod from Disney was a significant endorsement of their work. However, this also meant that the pressure to perform was immense, and the lack of direct encouragement could be demoralizing for some.

This duality in Disney's persona – publicly warm and charismatic, privately shy and reserved – illustrates the complexity of his character. He was a visionary leader who inspired those around him but also a deeply private individual who struggled with insecurity and shyness. This intricate balance between his public image and private self contributed to the enigmatic allure of Walt Disney, making him a figure of endless fascination and admiration.

Disney's life was a continuous interplay between these contrasting aspects of his personality. His ability to maintain this balance while achieving unparalleled success in the entertainment industry is a tribute to his extraordinary talent and resilience. Despite the personal challenges he faced, Disney's unwavering dedication to his work and his vision for the future left an unremovable mark on the world, ensuring that his legacy would endure long after his passing.

Walt Disney's reputation has indeed been the subject of polarized opinions over the decades. Early evaluations painted him as a patriot, folk artist, and popularizer of culture. He was celebrated for his contributions to the American entertainment industry, his innovations in animation, and his ability to create beloved characters and stories that resonated with audiences worldwide. Disney's work was seen as embodying the American spirit, with themes of optimism, hard work, and the pursuit of dreams.

However, more recent assessments have cast Disney in a less flattering light. Critics have described him as a model of American imperialism*

---

* Imperialism can be defined as a doctrine, political strategy, practice, state policy, or

and intolerance, arguing that his work promoted a very white and commercialized version of American culture that suppressed diversity and alternative viewpoints. Some view Disney as a cynical manipulator of cultural and commercial formulas, accusing him of creating content that, while outwardly wholesome, masked underlying themes of cultural dominance and commercial exploitation. These critics suggest that Disney's creations presented an overly simplistic and sanitized view of the world.

One of the most controversial aspects of Disney's legacy is the accusation of anti-Semitism. This criticism is partly rooted in an incident where Disney gave Nazi propagandist Leni Riefenstahl a tour of his studio shortly after Kristallnacht, a series of violent anti-Jewish pogroms in Nazi Germany. This event drew significant criticism, with many questioning Disney's judgment and possible sympathies. However, Disney's biographer Neal Gabler argues that Disney was apolitical during the 1930s, suggesting that he may not have fully grasped the implications of his actions.

Despite these accusations, Disney's actions during World War II paint a different picture. He demonstrated significant support for the United States' war efforts, producing propaganda films against the Nazis and offering his studio's services to various branches of the Armed Forces. These films, such as *Der Fuehrer's Face* and *Education for Death*, were designed to boost morale and educate the public about the dangers of Nazi ideology. Disney's contributions to the war effort suggest a strong anti-Nazi stance, conflicting with the accusations of anti-Semitism.

The Walt Disney Family Museum acknowledges that some early cartoons contained ethnic stereotypes that were common in films of the 1930s. These portrayals reflect the prejudices and insensitivities of the time rather than Disney's personal views. The museum also points out that Disney regularly donated to Jewish charities and was named the 1955 "Man of the Year" by the B'nai B'rith chapter in Beverly Hills. This organization found no evidence of anti-Semitism on

---

advocacy that consists in extending power by territorial acquisition or by extending political and economic control outward over other areas.

Disney's part, awarding him for exemplifying the best principles of American citizenship and inter-group understanding.

Many of Disney's employees, including several who were Jewish, have defended him against accusations of anti-Semitism. Animator Joe Grant, who worked closely with Disney, stated, "As far as I'm concerned, there was no evidence of anti-Semitism. I think the whole idea should be put to rest and buried deep." This sentiment is echoed by other employees who knew Disney personally and professionally, suggesting that the accusations may be based on misunderstandings or misinterpretations of his actions.

In addition to allegations of anti-Semitism, Disney has also faced accusations of racism due to some of his productions released between the 1930s and 1950s containing racially insensitive material. These films often included stereotypes and caricatures that are now widely recognized as offensive. However, many who worked with Disney, including Floyd Norman, the studio's first black animator, refuted these claims. Norman stated that he never observed any hint of racist behavior from Disney, emphasizing that Disney's treatment of people was exemplary and inclusive.

Disney's close friendship with James Baskett, the star of *Song of the South*, further challenges the accusations of racism. *Song of the South* has been criticized for its portrayal of African American characters and its romanticized view of the pre-civil war South. Despite these criticisms, Disney and Baskett developed a strong friendship during the film's production. Disney recognized Baskett's talent and campaigned successfully for Baskett to receive an Honorary Academy Award for his performance, making him the first black actor to be honored in this way. When Baskett's health declined, Disney provided financial support to him and his family, demonstrating his personal commitment and kindness.

These actions suggest a more nuanced view of Disney's character. While some of his work reflected the prejudices of his time, his personal relationships and professional decisions often contradicted the accusations of racism. Disney's legacy is complex, marked by both his groundbreaking contributions to entertainment and the controversies that have emerged over the years.

In examining Disney's reputation, it's essential to consider the context of his times and the broader cultural and social dynamics that influenced his work. While criticisms of his cultural impact and personal beliefs persist, Disney's innovations in animation, storytelling, and theme park design continue to be celebrated. His creations have brought joy to millions and have become an integral part of global popular culture.

Disney's ability to navigate and influence the entertainment industry, despite personal and professional challenges, underscores his enduring legacy. His commitment to pushing the boundaries of what was possible in entertainment, his visionary approach to storytelling, and his ability to create experiences that resonate across generations ensure that Walt Disney remains a significant figure in the history of entertainment. His legacy is a testament to the power of imagination, innovation, and the enduring appeal of stories that touch the hearts of people around the world.

Despite the controversies, Disney's contributions to the entertainment industry have been widely recognized and celebrated. He received fifty-nine Academy Award nominations, winning twenty-two, both records. Disney was also nominated for three Golden Globe Awards and received two Special Achievement Awards for *Bambi* and *The Living Desert*. Additionally, he won an Emmy Award for Best Producer for the *Disneyland* television series.

Several of Disney's films are included in the United States National Film Registry by the Library of Congress as "culturally, historically, or aesthetically significant," including *Steamboat Willie*, *The Three Little Pigs*, *Snow White and the Seven Dwarfs*, *Fantasia*, *Pinocchio*, *Bambi*, *Dumbo*, and *Mary Poppins*. In 1998, the American Film Institute published a list of the 100 greatest American films, which included *Snow White and the Seven Dwarfs* and *Fantasia*.

In February 1960, Disney was inducted into the Hollywood Walk of Fame with two stars, one for motion pictures and the other for his television work. Mickey Mouse was given his own star in 1978, and Disneyland received one in 2005. Disney was also inducted into the Television Hall of Fame in 1986 and the California Hall of Fame in 2006.

The Walt Disney Family Museum records that Disney, along with members of his staff, received more than 950 honors and citations from throughout the world. He was made a Chevalier* in the French Légion d'honneur in 1935 and received the country's highest artistic decoration, the Officer d'Academie, in 1952. Other national awards include Thailand's Order of the Crown, Germany's Order of Merit, Brazil's Order of the Southern Cross, and Mexico's Order of the Aztec Eagle. In the United States, Disney received the Presidential Medal of Freedom in 1964 and was posthumously awarded the Congressional Gold Medal in 1968.

Walt Disney's death marked the end of an era but also left behind a legacy that would continue to influence the world of entertainment for generations to come. After Disney's passing, his brother Roy O. Disney deferred his retirement to take full control of the Disney companies. Roy ensured that Walt's vision for Disney World and EPCOT (Experimental Prototype Community of Tomorrow) would be realized, dedicating the Magic Kingdom at Disney World to his brother when it opened in 1971. The dedication was a heartfelt tribute to Walt's dream and vision, encapsulating his belief in creating a place where families could come together and experience joy and wonder.

EPCOT Center, which opened in 1982, became a permanent world's fair rather than the functional city Walt had envisioned. Nonetheless, it served as a showcase for technological innovation and cultural exchange, reflecting Walt's belief in the potential of creativity and

---

* The term "chevalier" is derived from the French word for "knight," and historically, it refers to a member of a chivalric order or a knightly class.

progress. EPCOT was designed to inspire and educate visitors about the possibilities of the future, highlighting advancements in science, technology, and international cooperation. Although it deviated from Walt's original plan, EPCOT embodied his forward-thinking ideals and continued to promote a message of innovation and global unity.

The Walt Disney Family Museum, which opened in 2009, provides a comprehensive look at Disney's life and achievements, offering visitors a deeper understanding of the man behind the magic. The museum's extensive collection of artifacts and awards highlights Disney's impact on the entertainment industry and his enduring legacy. Located in the Presidio of San Francisco, the museum was designed by Disney's daughter Diane and her son, Walter E. D. Miller, ensuring that Walt's story was told with authenticity and depth. The exhibits chronicle Disney's journey from his early days to the creation of his iconic characters and theme parks, providing insight into his creative process and visionary leadership.

In the decades since Disney's death, the company he founded has continued to grow and evolve, maintaining the high standards of creativity and innovation that he established. Disney's influence can be seen in every aspect of the entertainment industry, from film and television to theme parks and beyond. His commitment to storytelling, technology, and imagination has left a lasting mark on the world, ensuring that his legacy will continue to inspire future generations.

Today, Disney's impact is evident in the global reach of The Walt Disney Company. The company has expanded its portfolio to include acquisitions of major franchises such as Pixar, Marvel, Lucasfilm, and 21st Century Fox, each bringing beloved characters and stories into the Disney fold. This expansion has allowed Disney to dominate the box office with blockbuster hits and continue to push the boundaries of animation and special effects. Films like *Toy Story*, *The Avengers*, and *Star Wars* are testament to the company's ongoing influence in the entertainment world.

Disney's theme parks have also grown, with new parks opening around the world, including in Tokyo, Paris, Hong Kong, and Shanghai. These parks continue to attract millions of visitors each year, offering immersive experiences that blend cutting-edge technology with the timeless magic of Disney storytelling. Innovations like Star Wars: Galaxy's Edge at Disneyland in California and Disney's Hollywood Studios in Florida, as well as the upcoming Avengers Campus at Disney California Adventure Park and Walt Disney Studios Park in Paris, illustrate Disney's commitment to creating unparalleled guest experiences. These attractions transport visitors to the worlds of their favorite films.

The company's foray into streaming with Disney+ has revolutionized how audiences consume content, offering a vast library of movies, TV shows, and exclusive original programming. Disney+ has quickly become a major player in the streaming wars, showcasing the company's ability to adapt to changing media landscapes and consumer preferences. This platform not only brings classic Disney content to new generations but also allows for the creation of new stories and series that expand beloved universes.

Disney's impact extends beyond entertainment. The company has become a leader in corporate social responsibility, with initiatives focused on environmental sustainability, community engagement, and charitable giving. Disney's commitment to reducing its environmental footprint is evident in its efforts to achieve net zero greenhouse gas emissions, reduce waste, and conserve water resources. Programs such as the Disney Conservation Fund support wildlife conservation projects around the globe, reflecting Walt's own passion for nature and the environment.

Furthermore, Disney's influence on popular culture is profound. Characters like Mickey Mouse, Cinderella, and Elsa have become cultural icons, recognized and beloved worldwide. Disney's stories and characters continue to inspire merchandise, theme park attractions, and even academic studies, illustrating their pervasive impact on society. The company's dedication to diversity and inclusion is also evident in its recent films and initiatives, striving to represent a broader range of voices and stories.

The influence of Walt Disney is felt in every corner of the entertainment industry and beyond. His pioneering work in animation set the standard for quality and storytelling that continues to guide the industry. Disney's vision of theme parks as immersive experiences laid the foundation for the modern theme park industry, influencing the design and operation of parks worldwide. His commitment to technological innovation paved the way for advancements in film, television, and interactive media.

In education, Disney's approach to combining entertainment with learning has inspired countless educational programs and materials that engage and educate students in creative ways. His belief in the power of storytelling to convey complex ideas and inspire curiosity remains a guiding principle in educational media.

In sum, Walt Disney's work continues to inspire new generations of artists, storytellers, and innovators, ensuring that the magic of Disney will live on for many years to come. Through his visionary leadership and relentless pursuit of excellence, Walt Disney transformed the entertainment industry and left an indelible mark on the world, a testament to the power of imagination and the enduring appeal of great storytelling.

Disney's commitment to storytelling, technology, and imagination has left a lasting mark on the world, ensuring that his legacy will continue to inspire future generations. His legacy lives on through the countless people who continue to be inspired by his creativity, innovation, and belief in the power of imagination.

# Conclusion

Walt Disney's life and legacy epitomize the power of imagination, innovation, and unyielding determination. From his humble beginnings in Chicago to the creation of a global entertainment empire, Disney's journey was marked by visionary achievements and an unwavering commitment to storytelling. His story is a model for the extraordinary impact one individual can have on the world, shaping not only an industry but also the cultural fabric of society.

Disney's pioneering spirit led to the creation of timeless characters like Mickey Mouse and unforgettable films that revolutionized animation. His ability to blend technical advancements with compelling narratives set new standards in entertainment, captivating audiences across generations.

The creation of Disneyland in 1955 was a bold venture that redefined family entertainment. Disney's vision of a magical, immersive environment where families could experience joy and wonder together became a reality, setting the stage for future theme parks around the world. Disneyland's success was a testament to Disney's ability to transform dreams into reality, providing a space where imagination could flourish.

Disney's contributions to the 1964 New York World's Fair, including attractions like "It's a Small World" and "Great Moments with Mr. Lincoln," highlighted his commitment to using technology to enhance storytelling and create meaningful experiences. These projects laid the groundwork for future innovations in theme park design and visitor engagement.

In his later years, Disney's ambitions extended to the creation of Disney World in Florida and the visionary EPCOT project. These endeavors reflected his belief in the potential of creativity and technology to shape a better future. Despite facing personal health challenges, Disney's passion and dedication remained undiminished, driving him to continue exploring new frontiers in entertainment.

Walt Disney's enduring legacy is evident in the countless films, theme parks, and cultural touchstones that continue to enchant and inspire people around the globe. His ability to dream big and his relentless pursuit of those dreams have left an indelible mark on the world. Disney's story is a reminder that with imagination, innovation, and perseverance, the extraordinary is always within reach.

As we reflect on the life of Walt Disney, we are reminded of the transformative power of creativity and the enduring impact of a visionary mind. Disney's journey from a small house on Tripp Avenue to becoming a global icon is a story of passion, resilience, and the belief that anything is possible. His legacy continues to inspire us to dream, to innovate, and to create worlds of wonder and joy for generations to come.

# Appendices

## Walt Disney: A Chronological Timeline

1901

• Walt Disney is born on December 5 in Chicago to Elias Disney and Flora Call Disney.

1906

• The Disney family moves to Marceline, Missouri, where Walt enjoys an idyllic childhood on a farm and develops a strong interest in drawing.

1910

- Due to poor health, Elias Disney sells the farm.

1917

• The Disney family moves to Chicago. Walt draws pictures for the McKinley High School newspaper and attends evening classes at the Chicago Academy of Fine Arts. He hopes to become a newspaper cartoonist.

1918

• Walt lies about his age to join the American Ambulance Corps and serves in France following the end of World War I.

1919

• Walt returns to the U.S., moves to Kansas City, and gets a job at the Pesmen-Rubin Commercial Art Studio for $50 a month.

1920

• Walt meets Ub Iwerks and forms Iwerks-Disney Commercial Artists. The company fails after one month. Walt and Iwerks get jobs with the Kansas City Slide Company (later KC Film Ad Company) and discover animation. Walt creates Newman Laugh-O-Grams, producing advertising and topical shorts, as well as story cartoons.

1922

• Walt incorporates Laugh-O-Gram Films, Inc. with $15,000 from backers.

1923

• Laugh-O-Gram goes bankrupt. Walt moves to Hollywood to become a director. With his brother Roy, he establishes the Disney Brothers Studio, landing a contract for the *Alice Comedies*, a series in which a young girl filmed in live action interacts with animated characters.

1924

• Walt hires animators, including Ub Iwerks, ceases animating, and focuses on story development and direction. Lillian Bounds, Walt's future wife, starts work at the studio as an inker.

1925

• Walt and Lillian get married.

1926

• Walt and Roy rename the studio Walt Disney Studios and move it to a new building on Hyperion Avenue, which later becomes known as the Hyperion Studio.

1927

• Film distributor Charles Mintz contracts Walt Disney Studios to create a new series of animation films based on Oswald the Lucky Rabbit. Mintz owns the rights to the character. When the series succeeds and Walt asks for a larger budget, Mintz asserts trademark rights and tries to take over Walt Disney Studios. Walt abandons the character to Mintz.

1928

• Walt creates Mickey Mouse. He produces Steamboat Willie, an innovative cartoon that synchronizes sound and animation. Mickey becomes a national sensation.

1929

• Walt launches *Silly Symphonies*, a series of cartoons that combine music and animation.

1930

• Roy and Walt Disney license Mickey-related merchandising.

1931

• Membership in the Mickey Mouse Club surpasses one million people.

1932

• Walt acquires exclusive use of three-strip Technicolor for cartoons and incorporates the technology into his films. He hires teachers from the Chouinard Art Institute to give classes at the studio.

1933

• *Three Little Pigs*, the 36th *Silly Symphony*, is distributed with the original song, *Who's Afraid of the Big Bad Wolf?* The song becomes a national hit and an anthem for the Great Depression. Lillian Disney gives birth to Diane Disney.

1936

• Lillian and Walt adopt Sharon Disney.

1937

• Disney Studios develops a sophisticated multiplane camera that gives depth to its films. The studio uses it in the *Silly Symphony*, *The Old Mill*, and in Disney's first feature-length animated film, *Snow White and the Seven Dwarfs*.

1938

• Walt's mother, Flora, dies.

1939

• Walt wins an honorary Academy Award with one full-sized Oscar and seven miniatures for *Snow White and the Seven Dwarfs*.

1940

• Disney releases *Pinocchio* and *Fantasia*. *Fantasia* is released with Fantasound, a precursor to stereo and surround sound. Neither film is commercially successful. Walt Disney Studios issued 600,000 shares of common stock at $5.00 per share, totaling $3,000,000. Adjusted for inflation, this amount is approximately $38,980,656 in today's money.

1941

• Disney Studios releases *Dumbo*, which is a modest commercial success. The animators at the studio strike and unionize. Walt goes on a goodwill tour in South America. The United States enters World War II; the U.S. Army requisitions half of Disney Studios to house troops assigned to protecting a nearby Lockheed plant. Walt's father, Elias, dies.

1942

• Disney Studios releases *Bambi*, its most naturalistic animation film to date, and *Saludos Amigos*, a movie for South American markets. *Bambi* is not commercially successful. Disney Studios begins making morale-boosting and propaganda films.

1944

• Disney re-releases *Snow White and the Seven Dwarfs* successfully.

1946

• Walt, who has provided Mickey Mouse's voice for nearly twenty years, reassigns the role for Fun and Fancy Free. The studio releases *Song of the South*, which enjoys commercial success.

1947

• James Baskett, who played Uncle Remus in *Song of the South*, wins an honorary Academy Award. Walt testifies before the House Un-American Activities Committee on the role of communist agitation in the 1941 animators strike at the studio.

1948

• Disney Studios premieres *Seal Island*, the first of the *True-Life Adventures* series, one of the film industry's earliest nature documentaries. Walt visits a railroad fair in Chicago and soon decides to create a railroad for his home.

1949

• *Seal Island* wins the Academy Award for best two-reel documentary.

1950

• *Cinderella* becomes Disney's first commercially successful animated feature since *Snow White and the Seven Dwarfs*. Disney releases *Treasure Island*, its first all-live-action movie.

1953

• Disney creates the Buena Vista Film Distribution Company.

1954

• Disney contracts with ABC television to produce a one-hour television program in exchange for a $500,000 investment by ABC in Disneyland. Walt buys 244 acres (10,625,280 square feet or 987,437 square meters) of land near Anaheim, California, to be the site for Disneyland.

1955

• *Lady and the Tramp* is the first animated feature filmed in wide-screen CinemaScope technology. Disneyland opens and receives over one million visitors within two months. Walt introduces the *Mickey Mouse Club* program on ABC.

1960

• Disney serves as Head of Pageantry of the 1960 Winter Olympics.

1961

• Walt and Roy establish plans to create the California Institute of the Arts through the merger of the Los Angeles Conservatory of Music and the Chouinard Art Institute.

1964

• *Mary Poppins* is released and later nominated for thirteen Academy Awards. President Lyndon B. Johnson presents Walt with the Presidential Medal of Freedom, the nation's highest civil honor. Walt, working in planning consultation with Robert Moses, designs four exhibits for the 1964-1965 World's Fair in New York City, including "It's a Small World."

1965

• Walt Disney Studios purchases land in Orlando, Florida for EPCOT, the Experimental Prototype Community of Tomorrow, which also leads to the creation of Walt Disney World.

1966

• Walt Disney dies on December 15.

# Fun Facts About Walt Disney

• In 1901, Walt Disney was born on the second floor of a wooden cottage designed and built by his parents in Chicago.

• Walt Disney once played Peter Pan in a school play.

• Disney dropped out of high school at sixteen to enlist in the Army but ended up volunteering with the Red Cross instead.

• Before founding his studio, Disney worked as an artist for a Kansas City advertising agency.

• Disney's first animation studio, Laugh-o-Gram, went bankrupt in less than a year.

• Oswald the Lucky Rabbit was Disney's first cartoon character, not Mickey Mouse.

• Walt Disney voiced Mickey Mouse from 1929 until 1947.

• Disney was once the only person allowed to create full-color Technicolor cartoons, a significant advantage that came from securing an exclusive contract with Technicolor.

• Walt Disney holds the record for the most Academy Awards won by an individual, with twenty-two awards.

• During World War II, Disney's studio produced propaganda cartoons for the U.S. government.

• Disney was an outspoken opponent of communism during the Cold War.

• Walt Disney received the Presidential Medal of Freedom from President Lyndon B. Johnson in 1964.

• Disney had a lifelong fascination with trains, building elaborate train sets and a miniature railroad at his home.

• The idea for Disneyland came to Disney while watching his daughters ride a merry-go-round at Griffith Park.

• Disney bought the land for Disney World under fake names to keep his identity secret.

• Disney had a secret apartment above the firehouse on Main Street, U.S., in Disneyland.

• Disney invented audio-animatronics, with the first figure being Abraham Lincoln at the 1964 World's Fair.

• Disney's housekeeper, Thelma Pearl Howard, became a multimillionaire thanks to the Disney stocks he gave her every year.

• Disney planned to open a major ski resort in Mineral King Valley, near Sequoia National Park, but the project was shelved after his death.

# Quotes by Walt Disney

"Art is never conscious. Things that have lived were seldom planned that way. If you follow that line, you're on the wrong track. We don't even let the word 'art' be used around the studio. If anyone begins to get arty, we knock them down. What we strive for is entertainment."

"Films stimulate children to read books on many subjects."

"I am not influenced by the techniques or fashions of any other motion picture company."

"Women are the best judges of anything we turn out. Their taste is very important. They are the theater-goers, they are the ones who drag the men in. If the women like it, to heck with the men."

"When people laugh at Mickey Mouse it's because he's so human; and that is the secret of his popularity."

"There is more treasure in books than in all the pirates' loot on Treasure Island and at the bottom of the Spanish Main… and best of all, you can enjoy these riches every day of your life."

"Everyone has been remarkably influenced by a book, or books. In my case, it was a book on cartoon animation. I discovered it in the Kansas City Library at the time I was preparing to make motion-picture animation for my life's work. The book told me all I needed to know as a beginner – all about the arts and the mechanics of making drawings that move on the theater screen. From the basic information, I could go on to develop my own way of movie storytelling. Finding that book was one of the most important and useful events in my life. It happened at just the right time. The right time for reading a story or an article or a book is important. By trying too hard to read a book that, for our age and understanding, is beyond us, we may tire of it. Then, even after, we'll avoid it and deny ourselves the delights it holds."

"If I can't find a theme, I can't make a film anyone else will feel. I can't laugh at intellectual humor. I'm just corny enough to like to have a story hit me over the heart."

"From years of experience, I have learned what could legitimately be added to increase the thrills and delights of a fairy tale without violating the moral and meaning of the original. Audiences have confirmed this unmistakably. We define the heroines and heroes more vividly; add minor characters to help carry the story line; virtually create such immortal friends of the heroine as the Seven Dwarfs. Storywise, we sharpen the decisive triumph of good over evil with our valiant knights − the issues which represent our moral ideals. We do it in a romantic fashion, easily comprehended by children. In this respect, moving pictures are more potent than volumes of familiar words in books."

"Disneyland is like Alice stepping through the looking glass; to step through the portals of Disneyland will be like entering another world."

"A word may be said in regard to the concept and conduct of Disneyland's operational tone. Although various sections will have the fun and flavor of a carnival or amusement park, there will be none of the 'pitches,' game wheels, sharp practices and devices designed to milk the visitor's pocketbook."

"On our first television program we showed you a blueprint for a dream. Well, this is the blueprint, and the dream is Disneyland, the park that we're constructing near Anaheim, California. We promised to keep you informed as our dream became a reality. So, for a firsthand progress report, let's visit Disneyland now. We could go by car, of course −it's a pleasant fifty-minute trip across town. But let's be different. Let's take to the air. Let's go by helicopter."

"Here in Florida, we have something special we never enjoyed at Disneyland… the blessing of size. There's enough land here to hold all the ideas and plans we can possibly imagine."

"Believe me, it's the most exciting and challenging assignment we have ever tackled at Walt Disney Productions."

"It is good to have a failure while you're young because it teaches you so much. For one thing, it makes you aware that such a thing can happen to anybody, and once you've lived through the worst, you're never quite as vulnerable afterward."

"Get a good idea, and stay with it. Dog it, and work at it until it's done, and done right."

"To some people, I am kind of a Merlin who takes lots of crazy chances, but rarely makes mistakes. I've made some bad ones, but fortunately, the successes have come along fast enough to cover up the mistakes. When you go to bat as many times as I do, you're bound to get a good average. That's why I keep my projects diversified."

"Naturally, we are all extremely gratified by the reception given Snow White, for it shows us conclusively that the public is ready for more animated features."

"People often ask me if I know the secret of success and if I could tell others how to make their dreams come true. My answer is you do it by working."

"Adults are interested if you don't play down to the little two or three-year-olds or talk down. I don't believe in talking down to children. I don't believe in talking down to any certain segment. I like to kind of just talk in a general way to the audience. Children are always reaching."

"Despite all the publicity about delinquency, America's youngsters are a pretty good lot. One of the things I want to do is make a picture that shows the good side of teenagers. I get so put out with all these pictures about delinquency. One picture upset me for three days afterward. I think these pictures are a mistake. Children get bad ideas when they see such things on the screen. And I don't think they show a true picture of young people today."

"You'll be a poorer person all your life if you don't know some of the great stories and the great poems. But the actual world of nature and human nature is where you will live and work with your neighbors and your competitors. So keep your eyes open."

"It has always been my hope that our fairy tale films will result in a desire of viewers to read again the fine old original tales and enchanting myths on the home bookshelf or school library. Our motion picture productions are designed to augment them, not to supplant them."

"Crowded classrooms and half-day sessions are a tragic waste of our greatest national resource —the minds of our children."

"Why do animals dominate animated cartoons? Because their reaction to any kind of stimulus is expressed physically. Often the entire body comes into play. Take a joyful dog. His tail wags, his torso wiggles, his ears flap. He may greet you by jumping on your lap or by making the circuit of the room, not missing a chair or a divan. He keeps barking, and that's a form of physical expression, too; he stretches his big mouth. But how does a human being react to a stimulus? He's lost the sense of play he once had and he inhibits physical expression. He is the victim of a civilization whose ideal is the unbotherable, poker-faced man and the attractive, unruffled woman. Even the gestures get to be calculated. They call it poise. The spontaneity of the animal, you find it in small children, but it's gradually trained out of them."

"Animals have personalities like people and must be studied."

"Throughout our career in motion pictures, classical music has played a very important part. Early in the beginning we created a cartoon series called Silly Symphonies… simple short subjects that relied heavily on the works of classical composers. The popularity of the Silly Symphonies led us to undertake a major effort, Fantasia, which featured the music of Bach, Dukas, Tchaikovsky, Stravinsky, Moussorgsky, Beethoven, and Schubert."

"I can never stand still. I must explore and experiment. I am never satisfied with my work. I resent the limitations of my own imagination."

"You know, there was once a time, and it wasn't too many years ago either, when any boy who was figuring on running away from home just naturally started dreaming about joining a circus."

"You don't build it for yourself. You know what the people want, and you build it for them."

"Deeds, rather than words, express my concept of the part religion should play in everyday life. I have watched constantly that in our movie work, the highest moral and spiritual standards are upheld, whether it deals with fables or with stories of living action."

"I ask myself, 'Live a good Christian life.' Toward that objective, I bend every effort in shaping my personal, domestic, and professional activities and growth."

"Christmas is bigger than all of us."

"I believe firmly in the efficacy of religion, in its powerful influence on a person's whole life. It helps immeasurably to meet the storm and stress of life and keep you attuned to the Divine inspiration. Without inspiration, we would perish."

"Nothing is ever born afraid… Young things – human and animal, boy or black lamb – have had no experience with fear. They rely implicitly on parents – lon someone bigger and stronger than themselves, to assure safety… on God as they grow older and threats to security multiply."

# References


Crowther, Bosley. *Walt Disney: American film producer*. Britannica (2024). https://www.britannica.com/biography/Walt-Disney. Accessed June 10th, 2024.

Hourly History. *Walt Disney: A Life From Beginning to End*. New York. CreateSpace Independent Publishing Platform, 2018.

Kampff, Joseph. *Walt Disney: Legendary Animator and Entertainment Entrepreneur*. New York. Rosen Publishing Group, Incorporated, 2015.

Korkis, Jim. *The Tri-Circle-D Story*. Mouse Planet (2014). https://mouseplanet.com/the-tri-circle-d-story/4310/. Accessed June 5th, 2024.

Korkis, Jim. *Walt and Lilly: A Disney Love Story*. Mouse Planet (2018). https://mouseplanet.com/walt-and-lilly-a-disney-love-story/6359/. Accessed June 12th, 2024.

Walter E. Disney, Staff of the Walt Disney Archives. *The Official Walt Disney Quote Book*. New York. Disney Publishing Worldwide, 2023.

Watts, Steven. *The Magic Kingdom: Walt Disney and the American Way of Life*. Columbia. Publisher, 2013.

Wikipedia. *Walt Disney*. Wikipedia (2024). https://en.wikipedia.org/wiki/Walt_Disney. Accessed June 8th, 2024.

# Thanks for reading!

As we close the final chapter of *A Brief History of Walt Disney*, I am grateful for the opportunity to embark on this personal journey with you through the pages of this book. Crafting this narrative has been a labor of love, driven by my deep reverence for Disney's remarkable life and enduring legacy. Each chapter is a testament to my dedication to illuminating the complexities of his story and the profound impact it continues to have on our understanding of creativity and human perseverance.

This book transcends mere historical documentation; it is a heartfelt tribute to Walt Disney's indomitable spirit and the timeless relevance of his contributions to entertainment and society. Countless hours of research and reflection have gone into capturing the essence of his experiences, as well as the broader historical context in which they unfolded. Through meticulous attention to detail and narrative nuance, I have endeavored to bring Disney's world vividly to life, inviting readers to immerse themselves in his journey of imagination, innovation, and entrepreneurial courage.

Your feedback is invaluable to me, serving not only as a reflection of your own engagement with the text but also as a guiding light for future readers. Whether you found inspiration in Disney's genius, were moved by his profound reflections, or have suggestions for how this work could be further enriched, I welcome your insights with an open heart and a deep sense of gratitude.

Please take a moment to share your thoughts and reflections by leaving a review. Your voice can shape the collective narrative of Disney's legacy and inspire others to embark on their own journey of discovery. Simply scan or click the QR code provided, which directs you to the Amazon page where you can leave your review. Your feedback is a vital contribution to our ongoing exploration of history's enduring lessons.

Thank you for joining me on this journey through the life and legacy of Walt Disney. May our shared appreciation for his story serve as a beacon of inspiration and understanding in an ever-changing world.

Warm regards,

Scott Matthews

# FIND MORE OF MY BOOKS ON AMAZON!

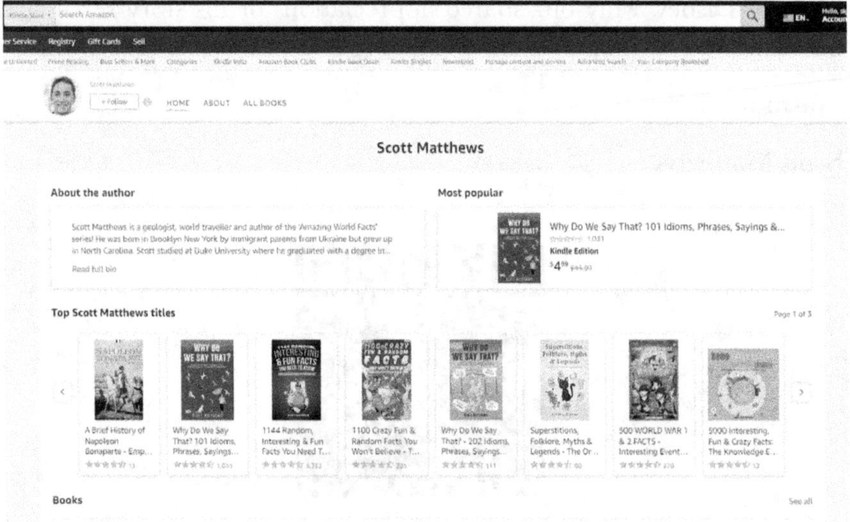

# DISCOVER MORE TITLES OF THE SERIES "A BRIEF HISTORY OF ..."!

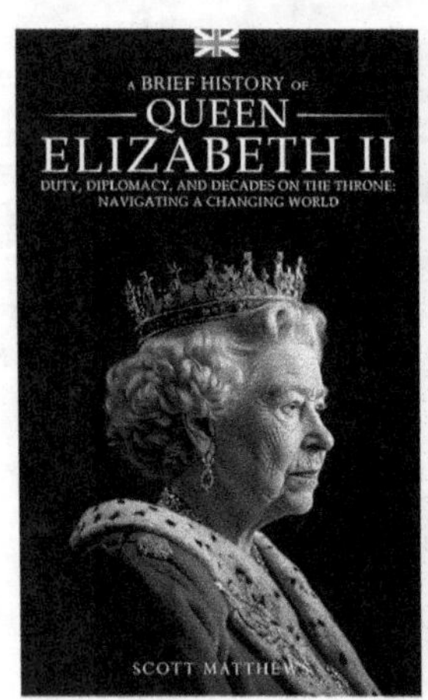

# EXPLORE THE "WHY DO WE SAY THAT" SERIES AND UNCOVER THE ORIGINS OF EVERYDAY IDIOMS AND PHRASES

### **Bonus!**

Thanks for supporting me and purchasing this book! I'd like to send you some freebies. They include:

- The digital version of *500 World War I & II Facts*

- The digital version of *101 Idioms and Phrases*

- The audiobook for my best seller *1144 Random Facts*

Scan the QR code below, enter your email and I'll send you all the files. Happy reading!